RETIREMENT

VILLAGE

BULLIES

Think before you buy!

ROBERTA CAVA

Copyright © 2014 by Roberta Cava

All rights reserved. No part of this work covered by the copyrights hereon may be reproduced or used in any form or by any means - graphic, electronic or mechanical, including photocopying, recording, taping or information storage and retrieval systems - without the prior written permission of the publisher.

Retirement Village Bullies

Think before you buy!

Roberta Cava

Published by Cava Consulting
105 / 3 Township Drive,
Burleigh Heads, 4220, Queensland, Australia
info@dealingwithdifficultpeople.info

Discover other titles by Roberta Cava at
www.dealingwithdifficultpeople.info

National Library of Australia

Cataloguing-in-publication data:

ISBN 978-0-9924489-0-5

BOOKS BY ROBERTA CAVA

Dealing with Difficult People

(21 publishers – in 16 languages)

Dealing with Difficult Situations – at Work and at Home

Dealing with Difficult Spouses and Children

Dealing with Difficult Relatives and In-Laws

Dealing with Domestic Violence and Child Abuse

Dealing with School Bullying

Dealing with Workplace Bullying

What am I going to do with the rest of my life?

Before tying the knot – Questions couples Must ask each other Before they marry!

How Women can advance in business

Survival Skills for Supervisors and Managers

Human Resources at its Best!

Human Resources Policies and Procedures - Australia

Employee Handbook

Easy Come – Hard to go – The Art of Hiring, Disciplining and Firing Employees

Time and Stress – Today's silent killers

Take Command of your Future – Make things Happen

Belly Laughs for All! – Volumes 1 to 4

Wisdom of the World! The happy, sad and wise things in life!

That Something Special

Retirement Village Bullies

RETIREMENT VILLAGE BULLIES
Think before you buy!

Table of Contents

Introduction	7
Chapter 1: February, 2007	9
Chapter 2: March, 2007	22
Chapter 3: April - July, 2007	27
Chapter 4: August, September and October, 2007	31
Chapter 5: November, 2007	35
Chapter 6: December, 2007	44
Chapter 7: January, 2008	62
Chapter 8: February, 2008	86
Chapter 9: March, 2008	112
Chapter 10: April, 2008	130
Chapter 11: May, 2008	169
Chapter 12: June, 2008	189
Conclusion	192
Notes *	193

INTRODUCTION

I had no knowledge about how a Retirement Village operated until I met a man who lived in one. I learned that the village property (including the land under the homes) was owned by a management firm who set the rules governed by the Queensland Retirement Village Act 1999 that heavily favoured the village land owners and not the retired people who had bought the properties on it.

The residents had to pay for their homes (most between $400,000 and $500,000 in value and because they didn't own the land they were not able to obtain a mortgage so had to pay cash for their dwellings). In addition they paid a residency fee per month to the management firm.

If residents found that they did not like their neighbours, became too ill to live in their home or didn't like the environment of the village, they would have to forfeit up to 30% of the value of their property PLUS 50% of the capital gain since purchasing their home if they chose to sell their unit. Although most of the residents had taken their option to buy to a lawyer, most of these lawyers were not aware of the hold the management firm would have on their everyday lives.

For instance, if an additional person was to stay in their unit overnight, they had to report this to the management firm. Management's reasoning for this was that they needed to know this information in case there was an emergency in the village. However, the residents did not have to tell them when they were **not** home overnight, so the management would not know whether anyone was home if there was some kind of emergency. So this ruling was rather pointless and embarrassing to those couples wanting to visit overnight.

The problems began when one of the residents lost his wife to cancer, started dating another woman and learned he had to let 'mother' (the management firm) know every time she stayed overnight. Serious problems started when the couple decided to live together in his unit.

Thanks to modern technology and emails I am able to give you a day-by-day account of the atrocities done by the Operators of the Retirement Village.

I have used an alias [Martin Williams] instead of the actual name of my partner throughout the book to protect his identity.

'Bad things happen when good people do nothing.'

Edmund Burke (1729 – 1793); and

The world suffers a lot, not because of the actions of bad people but because of the silence of good people!

(Author unknown)

CHAPTER 1

FEBRUARY, 2007

I'd been single for many years and occasionally used on-line dating services to meet compatible men. Because I am a best-selling author, do seminars world-wide and having a unique name, I am careful not to reveal my real name on the dating site because in the past I've been stalked by a man who wouldn't take 'no' for an answer.

There are other people involved in this story, so I will begin by itemising events as they occurred from February 2007 until June, 2008. Many of them involved emails and I have quoted verbatim from them.

16 February – my friends Sandy and George Latka (who live in Seba Beach in Alberta, Canada) arrived on the Gold Coast of Queensland. We met after they had settled into their hotel in Coolangatta.

20 February– I had been friends with Babette Davidson for several years. Her partner, Doug Johnson (a 6'3' man) had been in the hospital. He had fought and won his battle against pancreatic cancer in 1996, but was having the same symptoms again. He rallied and held off having further treatment at this time. His slim frame had shrunk noticeably by this time.

25 February

I had been listed on the on-line dating site RSVP and had met several men. However none seemed to fit until I received a 'Kiss' from Martin Williams. His description read as follows:

Looking for a toy boy? Sorry, I have passed my sell by date! But, if you are looking for a gentleman to treat you with courtesy and respect, look no further!

I am tall, active and physically fit, retired professional engineer of smart appearance who is sensitive, compassionate, well mannered, tolerant and caring, with a lively sense of humour, modern outlook (whilst retaining old fashioned morals of common decency) and an enthusiasm for life in general. I am widely travelled and have lived and worked in many countries. My hobbies are computer (mainly for photography) reading, gardening, and looking after my two loveable Siamese cats (love me, love my cats!).

I love the outdoors and enjoy day trips in the cooler season, sightseeing, long walks (beach and mountain preferred) travel in general, although I am quite happy and content with home life. Recently enjoyed a Red Centre holiday including The Ghan to Darwin. Next the Kimberley's!)

I became a widower just over two years ago after 44 years of marriage, so I think that shows a good sense of commitment ... a factor that seems to be missing in many of today's relationships.

I do like humour, friendship, trust, honesty, good manners, good food and healthy eating (cooking is my new passion) romantic dinners with a glass of wine, affection, dancing, driving, theatre and quiet periods of relaxation and meditation.

I do not like bad manners, selfishness, aggression, cruelty to animals and being taken for granted.

To sum up – a very lively young at heart self-funded retiree who loves life and want to share it with a lively companion.

Want to know more? Send me a kiss, or better still, an email.

Because my real name is rather unique and I'm well-known in some circles, I used my maiden name on the email site where answers were sent. Here is the following correspondence between us:

25 February – 11:37 am - he sent a 'kiss' and following message:

Hello lady with a lovely smile,

Upon recently rejoining RSVP, I was drawn to your profile and despite being older than your presumed maximum age preference, felt that there may be an underlining compatibility of interests – especially as the compatibility rating (if you believe it) is given as 80%!! I also have to say that I like your smile – hence this contact.

My name is Martin and I became a widower just over two years ago after 44 years of marriage. I joined RSVP a year ago because I 'thought' I needed to find a new soul-mate, but after a few 'coffee' meetings with RSVP contacts, realised that I was not ready to consider a new relationship, so withdrew my details.

I have now come to terms with living on my own, and strangely enough, feel very comfortable, enthusiastic and happy with my life. However, I realise that I miss the companionship of a partner to enjoy all the good things, such as sightseeing and holidays. Having meals on one's own does not have that same enjoyment. I also find dining, or spending a weekend with old friends who knew my wife rather difficult.

A very condensed background of my life is that I completed a full career as an engineer in the British army ending up as a commissioned officer. I then joined an electronics company in 1978 as a Logistics Manager for a communications project and finished up as a Technical Administration and Security Manager. I then set up my own business prior to migrating to Australia in 2000 to be closer to my daughter and grandchildren who became Australian citizens in 1988. The loss of my very lovely and vibrant wife in 2004 to breast cancer after 20 months of illness leading to full disability was a very traumatic period for all of us.

I own my own home and am a self-funded retiree – albeit with pensions from the UK. My daughter's partner built a holiday property on North Stradbroke Island and I have free reign to use the facility which has superb beach views. I love the solitude of Point Lookout and enjoy both interior bush walks and long walks along the various beaches – preferably in the cooler season – but so much nicer with a companion to share and enjoy the solitude, plus sit on the balcony in the evening with a glass of wine.

You will note from my profile that I have two cats and your preference was 'like pets but do not have any.' Sorry about that, but they came with us from the UK and were my wife's pride and joy, such that I was made to promise to look after them after she had passed over. They are now eleven years old, very affectionate and do not go outside the confines of house and garden. Not too much of a tie to my going out for the day or taking holidays.

I understand you will be given a link to my profile with this email and I know you are given a free reply, so if you feel that you would like to process this initial contact, I would be delighted and honoured to talk to you (telephone number please – or use mine 555-5555 if you are reluctant to release yours). However, if you would like to talk face to face over a cup of tea or coffee, please let me know. I have GPS navigation in my car so can find shopping centres etc.

I do hope I have piqued your curiosity!!

My regards and best wishes,

Martin

25 February at 2:15 pm I replied,

Hello Martin,

You have piqued my curiosity! I was pleased to receive your 'kiss' and even more pleased to see we are more compatible than the majority of men I have met through the dating service.

Like you, I immigrated to Australia, but from Canada in 1998 – a couple of years before you arrived.

I have been divorced for many years so have no baggage – in fact I'm probably too independent for my own good! Sorry to hear you lost your wife after such a successful marriage – that must have taken a long time to get over. Congratulations on trying again. Hope your daughter and her family agree that it's time for you to 'get on with your life.' This doesn't take anything away from the feelings you had for your wife – nobody can replace her!

One of my sons (I have two) is an electronic engineering technologist – works for a pipeline in Canada. He lives in Edmonton, Alberta and does ski patrolling as a hobby. My second son lives in Winnipeg, Manitoba – my daughter in Kelowna (Big White ski area in the Okanagan valley of British Columbia). So they are scattered around Canada. They are all married and between them they have four granddaughters. I travel back to Canada once or twice a year. I'll likely go back in July and Christmas this year. It's been a few years since I spent a Christmas there.

Like you, I've been self-employed (in my case since 1982). I've been trying to retire for a couple of years, but my clients simply won't let me. And the fact that I love what I do makes it harder and harder to stop. I do a considerable amount of travel to SE Asia as well, but my clients supply a four or five star hotel room, so I often have a friend or family member stay with me while I'm there. I have a three-week stint coming up in Bangkok, Kuala Lumpur and Singapore in May. So you see, I am away a lot, but keep in touch with my friends via the internet.

I was pleased to see that you have access to the unit in Stradbroke Island – it's far closer than Brisbane for a commute.

Regarding cats – I simply love them and would have one, but it wouldn't be fair to one to be left behind so often while I travel. I used to dog-sit a Jack Russell dog as well and just loved it! I am an animal nut. One of daughter-in-laws, Sue, is a Vet.

You can communicate with me via my hotmail address: (gave email address)

I would love to meet you.

Best regards,

Robbie

(A few hours later that day I received the following email: 3:47 pm)

Hello again Robbie,

Thank you for your very informative and friendly response to my original email. I am almost at a loss for words ... I could not believe that I have contacted such an interesting, positive and fascinating lady with so many interests in common. I agree wholeheartedly with your sentiments and would love to meet you too! I believe we have a lot to talk about and, without trying to pre-judge any outcome, have a feeling that we would be comfortable in each other's company.

I envy you your trip to Bangkok, KL and Singapore in May. I think Singapore is one of the cleanest and most exciting cities I have visited. I particularly like dining out at Clarke' Quay (The Lotus Flower) and would like to spend more time on Sentosa Island ... my wife and I had to cancel a five-day holiday there in 2001. As for Canada ... how could you possibly leave there? Again I envy you as this is a country we always wanted to visit and had started to make plans to do the tourist visit to Vancouver, the Rockies and Alaska Cruise, but the dreaded cancer struck before we could go. I have not been able to have the courage to do the trip on my own since. I suppose it is always better to be with a companion to fully share and enjoy the experience. I would imagine you really look forward to visiting your children and grandchildren at least once a year ... and this year ... Christmas in the snow!

My daughter (Lorna) works on a contract for BID as a technical author and until recently, attended meetings and seminars in Bangkok, South Africa, Chicago, Montreal and London with business class travel. The company has now been taken over by a

German firm who have curtailed all travel for the time being, so she is not too happy!

Thank you for your thoughtful condolences on the loss of my wife. As you say, nobody can replace her, but I firmly believe that there is someone else with whom I can have a long loving relationship ... it's just a case of finding the right one? I still have plenty of years left in me, so I am in no desperate hurry. Lorna and the grandchildren are fully supportive and my wife left strict instructions that I must find someone else, but told my Lorna that if she allowed me to marry an 'old crow' she would come back and haunt her ... not me! There is more humour to that story that will tell you some time.

Like you, I have no baggage but do have some immigration problems at present. Having been forced to give up my consultancy business upon leaving the UK, I envy you running your own business. Under the terms of my 'Aged Parent' (what a dreadful picture that terminology generates!!) visa 410, I am not allowed to carry out any form of employment in Australia until I am formally granted residency ... still some three years away at the present rate of annual acceptance by the immigration department!!! As a result, I have now moved from my original 410 Aged Parent visa to a Bridging visa with the restriction that if I leave Australia on holiday, I cannot get back in!! There are ways around this, providing I pay for a special exit/entry visa, but it is very restrictive for ad-hoc travel overseas. Despite this, the ATO are very quick to hit me for tax without any of the benefits afforded to Australian pensioners.

Robbie, I would really enjoy meeting you at a place of your choosing and am free most days except Wednesdays. I have so many questions to ask you and so much to tell you, but I would be quite happy to restrict our first meeting to a coffee and/or walk. I am not too familiar with the Gold Coast (have been into the hinterland quite a few times) but I do know the Harbour Town shopping precinct and Sanctuary Cove, plus I have GPS navigation and find anywhere else you might like, especially if you are living South of Burleigh Heads.

By the way, don't be surprised if my profile becomes hidden on RSVP ... I have to take it off occasionally to avoid kisses from ladies (some as low as 35 years) in Asia who are looking for Australian residency ... little do they know?

Thank you again for your informative response. I do look forward to meeting you and you have my telephone number should you wish to evaluate my voice prior to meeting.

Kind regards,

Martin

I replied at 4:50 pm

Hi Martin,

Two letters in one day – how lucky can I be? Yes, we will have lots to talk about.

Re: Singapore – I was just there from January 16th till 27th. I seem to be getting lots of contracts to work there lately. I was also there in September and November last year as well. I will be doing keynote talks to large groups of women in Bangkok, KL and Singapore the week of May 7th – then will do two weeks (8 full days of seminars) for my usual training firm there. I was going to go to Sentosa on my last trip, but unfortunately I got a dose of Montezuma's revenge (diarrhoea) so didn't want to go too far away from a ladies' room! I thought it was all the MSG they put in the food, and of course because I didn't want to get dehydrated, I drank a lot of water. It wasn't until I got home that I realised that it could have been the water (that has normally been very safe.) You can't imagine how difficult it was doing seminars with that kind of problem. Nobody was the wiser though and everything went well.

I too have wanted to go on an Alaska cruise – should have done so when I lived there – but will try to do so to coincide with one of my trips back to see my family. The Rockies are truly spectacular and take my breath away every time I get close to them. My son Mike's ski chalet is in Kelowna (where his sister lives) which is world-renowned for the skiing. Christmas has not been the same here – that's the only time I miss the snow and cold of Canada! It also reminds me of all the fun I had cross-country skiing (do not do the downhill stuff).

You mention that Lorna is a technical author – what does that mean? Does she write books or periodicals? It sounds as if she does her share of travelling as well.

Hopefully you will find a suitable 'young crow.'

It sounds as if Australia is being difficult with your residency. Are you not allowed to go out of Australia? Can't you get a permit to have multi-entry? I was able to do that before I emigrated. Surely they know that you won't take work away from an Australian? Or is it that they're worried that you might want a pension? With reciprocal agreements with Canada and Great Britain, they shouldn't care whether you are here or there. I get a full Canadian pension, because we have a different system and the money in my pension was put there by me! So it's my own money I'm living on – no means test at all. Australia could benefit if they used the Canadian plan.

It's time for me to get busy preparing my dinner.

Best regards,

Robbie

That evening at 8:55 pm he replied again

Hi Robbie,

At the risk of giving you a big head, I have decided to send you three letters in one day!! Please don't expect this as the norm ... my typing speed is too slow!!

I would be very pleased to meet you at Harbour Town on Tuesday at, say 10:30 am outside the Dimmey's? I presume this is the area where there are several Cafe's around a waterfall (now switched off) at the top of the street giving entrance to the cinemas? If not, I will arrive early to have a quick walk around to spy out the location. If all else fails and we miss each other, I would suggest the Colorado Store at 10:40. I know that since that extra street went in a couple of years ago, I cannot remember the different locations so easily. My mobile number (which I don't use too often except for emergency) is (he gave his number) and I will have it switched on ... providing you have one too?? Let me know what you think.

Lorna has a contract to write technical publications on the safety and use of the various gases manufactured and packaged (cylinders) by the BID Company Worldwide. Prior to joining the Ganet Company as a Logistics Manager, I had two years as a technical author, so perhaps it runs in the family.

I shall be interested to hear about the subject matter of your seminars around the World. You seem to be a very intelligent and competent lady ... as well as being rather attractive, if the photos are anything to go by. I shall also be interested in how your pension from Canada is paid ... mine are subject to the monthly rate of exchange between the AUD and Sterling ... quite a variation at times. I will also explain the immigration constrictions in more detail when we meet ... can't wait ... you have really piqued my curiosity.

Quite a memorable day and I am pleased that I had the courage to contact you and for your very upbeat responses. Thank you for that.

Sleep well and kind regards, Martin

26 February 9:15 am

Hi Martin,

What a lovely surprise to see your email when I woke up this morning. I hadn't checked my emails last night. (I type about 90-wpm so have no problem writing and writing and writing ...)

Glad to see someone else in Australia uses their mobile only for emergency situations, or when they want people to be able to contact them. People think I'm nuts, but I seldom have mine on. I will put it on though on Tuesday morning! My number is (gave number). I had to look it up – had no idea what it was. I'll have your number with me as well in case we miss each other.

Dimmey's is at the end of the shopping centre that has a McDonald's restaurant outside the entrance. The coffee shop is to the left and Dimmey's is to the right. I haven't been there for over a year, so hope my memory is correct. It seems to me they have Devonshire tea???

When I was in Canada, I marketed other trainers – one was a safety expert who did seminars on how to work in dangerous confined areas (where gasses and chemicals might be). He did all kinds of workplace safety sessions.

I have just got off MSN with my son Mike in Edmonton. He plans to spend two weeks at his chalet at Big White (Kelowna B.C.) starting mid-March. It will probably be the last of the snow, so he will want to enjoy as much skiing as he can. His wife Sue and daughter Jill will fly out on the 25th because of school spring break. They will be able to spend time with my daughter Michele and her family, but unfortunately the kids in British Columbia have a different time for spring break, so her kids will be in school.

I'm hoping to get all my kids and grand kids together when I come in July, but don't know whether my son Brian and family from Winnipeg will be able to come. That will be summer holidays from school so it depends on their work schedules whether they can get time off or not.

I will tell you all about my seminars when we meet.

I too have the Canadian amount (for my pension) converted into Aussie dollars and find the amounts fluctuate month to month. I was surprised to find that I qualified for the senior's medical coverage – have used it for prescriptions.

See you tomorrow. I'll be wearing a white skirt and black top so you should be able to spot me quite easily. My photo was just taken in December, so I look like my picture.

Till then, Robbie

Later that afternoon: 2:50 pm

Hi Robbie,

Many thanks for your very newsy letter ... I think I might wear the same as you for our meeting tomorrow – less the skirt of course!! ... black top and white (beige) longs (dare not show you my legs at this stage) unless the weather is forecast to be very hot, in which case I may wear shorts!!

I think I know the area where Dimmey's is located, so should have no problem finding it. My photos are also fairly recent so I think we will recognise each other straight away. I have loaded your phone number into my mobile and will call if there are delays on the motorway.

Have you had many RSVP meetings and do you look forward to them? I have had several and often find it hard to curb my expectations that 'this will be the one!' only to be quite disappointed. Having said that, I have met some very nice ladies, but not compatible to consider for a long-term friendship, or relationship. I am trying to approach tomorrow with a very open mind, but am finding it rather difficult not to prejudge the situation when you write such lucid and interesting letters – I am getting quite a buzz just at the thought of talking to you. Anyway Robbie, no matter what the future holds, I am sure we will have an enjoyable meeting and I will certainly enjoy being in the company of a very attractive lady.

Best regards, Martin

27 February – Martin drove from Wellington Point and we met at Harbour Town Shopping Centre and had coffee.

I was impressed by Martin's calmness and impeccable manners and his lean body, aristocratic and somewhat military bearing. He was very articulate and interesting to listen to. Martin Williams and his wife Anita decided to move to Australia from England in 2001 using an Australian Immigration Aged Parent visa to spend their retirement years closer to their daughter Lorna and her family. They bought a lovely three-bedroom villa in Wellington Manor, a large retirement village in Birkdale, Queensland that was still under construction.

The eighty or so village residents at that time voted to become the Wellington Manor Residents Association Inc. and in December 2001, Martin was elected president. For the next two years, Martin and the members of his committee expended a tremendous amount of time and energy in obtaining benefits and improvements from the then village operators, Manor Group Pty Ltd. The association encouraged residents and new arrivals into the village to organise regular sporting and social activities. The introduction of a weekly happy hour became a major social event. Now seven years later with a population of around 240 residents, the village is a vibrant and active community where volunteer residents organise a host of regular functions and activities.

In 2004, one enterprising resident organised a small group of male volunteers (of whom Martin is a member) to prepare and serve a two-course gourmet dinner calling the evening 'Master Chef Dinner' at $5.00 a head for around 100 residents, thus giving the ladies a night off. The fellows cooked, served and cleaned up after. This was expanded to include fish and chips for a monthly film night, a Sunday Western and chow night, Trivia night and more recently, a bi-monthly Sunday 'brekkie.' He described it as a happy time for the village residents and a fun place to live.

Martin's wife died in late 2004 after a long battle against breast cancer. The village residents rallied and did their best to help him through his bereavement. During the latter stages of his wife's illness, Martin resigned as president. He had to stop much of his volunteer work but slowly but surely he pitched in and began living life again.

He described his two male cats that he had promised his wife to care for after her death. They were getting on in years, but were basically healthy animals.

He seemed to be a very caring person and showed impeccable manners as he showed all the male courtesies towards a woman – pulling out her chair, opening the car door etc.

I felt very comfortable with him and broke one of my cardinal rules and took him to my home in Varsity Lakes. My unit overlooked a lake and we took a stroll around it and even threw a few crusts of bread to the ducks that came clambering for food. We talked the afternoon away. I cooked lunch and later that afternoon Martin left for the forty-five minute drive back to his home.

Shortly after he left, I sent an email to my long-time friend Pat in Canada and said 'I think he's a keeper!'

27 February 11:04 pm

Hi Roberta,

Just a quick note to say how much I enjoyed your company today and for allowing me into your home. You have certainly given me a lot to think about.

I had a surprisingly clear run home and was back by 6:20 pm in time to feed the boys, have a quick bite and then go down to play pool. The big talking point was a letter to all residents telling us that the Manor Group have sold Cleveland Manor and Wellington Manor (his village) Retirement Villages to a new conglomerate. There is a face to face information meeting this Friday morning, so things could get a bit lively.

Thanks again for your company today and please let me know when you have a day free to pop up to see my home.

Best wishes, Martin

CHAPTER 2
MARCH, 2007

1 March (Thursday) Email from Martin and my replies:

Hi Roberta,

Thanks for your response and I am pleased that you are thinking of paying me a visit. Friday is not a good day because the meeting starts at 10:30 and is likely to carry on well past midday with some 200 angry residents having their say. Also there is a further 'residents only' meeting at 5:00 pm.

So, Roberta, if you are in agreement and able to drive up here on Sunday, I will do my best to make you very welcome. I thought a short drive around the local area and a walk on the sand at Wellington Point, followed by lunch, would be the order of the day, so wear shorts and bring a change of shoes, just in case.

Sounds great – will do.

A Thai dinner in the evening is probably out of the question at this time as I doubt you would want to drive home in the dark ... or is that my male chauvinist protection coming out??

No – you are right. Things look so different at night, that my first trip I should travel in the daylight.

Hopefully there will be other times as I am certainly not getting cold feet at this early stage of our relationship – in fact I really enjoy being with an attractive lady with sharp intelligence who knows exactly where she is going and is comfortable with her independence. I wonder if that independence will be a barrier ... time will tell.

If you are able to come on Sunday, the code for the gate is (gave number) and I live at the top end of Court 31.

You haven't given me your unit # and exact address – which would be helpful to have that so I can find your unit.

Alternatively, call me when you get close and I will walk down to the gate.

I might have to do that if I get lost in the complex.

Best wishes (I had a good nose around your website – still no cold feet!)

Regards, Martin

I will phone you on Sunday just before I leave so you will have an idea when I will be arriving.'

Cheers,

Roberta

2 March (Friday) - Martin came to the Gold Coast and we had dinner with Babette, Doug, Sandy and George – had a wonderful evening with him and my friends.

March 4 (Sunday) - I drove to Martin's place. We met at Wellington Point beach area, went for a walk along the seashore and enjoyed lunch at the restaurant. Then I followed him in my car as he drove to his villa in the Wellington Manor Retirement Village.

We entered the complex and drove into Martin's driveway. It was pristine and beautifully kept. The bungalow was made of a lovely pale beige brick with a nicely designed white iron railing separating the front garden from the home. In front of that, next to the concrete driveway were several large potted trees and other potted plants in a bed of white stones.

To the left of the entranceway was the large master bedroom with its own full bathroom and walk-in closet. The hallway from the entranceway led to the back of the unit where Martin had a small office on the left, a full bathroom in the centre and a second bedroom to the right. As we made a sharp turn to the right at the entranceway I could see right through to the courtyard at the back of the home. To the right of the entranceway was the lounge and media room with comfortable chairs and loveseat. Martin showed me his large collection of DVD movies.

Further down the hallway was a large fish tank with many lovely fish. Just past that was a jungle gym for cats and upon it perched Martin's beautiful Siamese male cats Roger and Kona. To the left, down a short hallway was his dining room that looked out onto the courtyard. Just past that hallway were the kitchen on the left and the family room on the right. Off the family room was the laundry with an entrance to the back courtyard on one side and into the garage on the other. The kitchen featured an opening in the wall where food and necessities could be passed through for when dinners were held in the dining room. Martin explained that he usually ate at the glass-topped table in the family room that was just off the kitchen.

The courtyard was lovely with most of it covered by opaque ceiling. There were many lovely plants and a bubbling water feature that came out of three copper coloured pots. The courtyard had curved metal railings that kept the cats from escaping from the unit. Everything was tastefully furnished and immaculate. He regularly had a cleaning lady come to help with the housekeeping. He explained that each unit had a medic alert button in case any of the residents had a medical emergency.

Martin took me on a tour of the facilities. The recreation building was huge and was divided into many rooms. The main was an auditorium with a stage and sound system. There was a bar and fairly large kitchen off that room and the residents held many activities there. The side rooms were used for meetings, for arts and crafts, for playing cards etc. and a library There was also an office for the management group.

Outside the auditorium was another gathering area where food could be served to one hundred or more people. Nearby was a rather large swimming pool that had a ramp for wheelchairs to allow disabled residents the joy of being in the water. The grounds were tastefully decorated with many types of flowers and trees. Behind the units was a charming nature walk where Martin said he had seen several Koalas and other wildlife.

Martin was quite an accomplished cook and made our dinner that night. Then it was time for me to go, because I didn't want to be driving at night in a new environment.

11 March (Sunday)

Hi Roberta,

Sorry if I have given you the impression of not wanting to see you because of other 'mares or fillies' as it is certainly not the case ... as you know, I have withdrawn my profile from RSVP to avoid any further contacts and have only one other lady from the past who remains in contact as a friend.

Thanks for explaining that.

Although I did have things to do last Friday and over the weekend, I do have to be honest and say that I am not keen on driving down to the Gold Coast for brief meetings at a club, or noisy venue, and then driving home a couple of hours later for three reasons:

- *My hearing defect makes conversation very difficult in the noisy club scene and it is embarrassing not to hear questions and comments clearly (Martin wears hearing aids in both ears – caused by gunfire when he was in the army).* I should have realised this myself. I sometimes can't hear myself think in those environments!

- *Conversation with a group of friends means that I have little chance to talk directly to you and get to know you better.* Good point.

- *It is difficult to relax and have a couple of drinks because of driving home on the motorway at a time of night when idiots prevail!* Very true – that is my concern about either of us going out at night and having to drive home.

So far, we have not really discussed what we are looking for in our relationship and how we feel about each other after our three meetings and what problems would need to be faced if we continue into the future, plus we need to discuss some of our (my) fears in much more depth ... you must realise that you quite rightly emanate the aura of a very confident and successful lady and the fact that you are also very attractive gives me the impression that you do not need a man in your life on equal terms. The word equal is important because I cannot match your earning power at the present time. Am I being oversensitive? We need to be very open about this!

The difference between us money-wise is that yours is tied up in real estate – mine is in superannuation. This allows me to have more capital to do things. And remember, all the travelling I do is usually paid for by my clients – only my trips to Canada are not paid by them

Roberta, if you are willing, I would like to pick you up at around 10:00 am on say Thursday 15th and take you to Springbrook Mountains for some sightseeing, lunch and one-on-one conversation. Alternatively, we could go down the coast, just as long as we have a full day together. Please let me know if this date is not suitable, but also please say 'yes' to the proposal of a day out.

Sounds like a good plan. Let's do it!

Looking forward to hearing from you,

Cheers, Martin

13 March (Tuesday) 8:36 pm

Hi Roberta,

I tried calling your mobile number earlier, but it must be switched off and I didn't leave a message because I have some trouble hearing clearly at this location and the voice keeps breaking up. I went through all of our past emails and realise that I do not have your home phone number as I hear much better using landlines. I wanted to talk to you about the dates of your seminars in May because I have some Emirates frequent flyer points that I must use up before they expire and had a sudden thought about the possibly of meeting you in Singapore if you wanted some company in the evenings for dinner during the latter stages of your seminars ... food for thought?

If you are interested, we can talk about this on Thursday ... I have my fingers crossed that the weather will be fine and shine kindly upon our day out together ... I am looking forward to seeing you again.

I hope you have had a good day and appreciating today's cooler weather.

Best wishes, Martin

15 March, (Thursday)

Martin came and drove us to Springbrook – I made dinner – Martin drove home.

19 March (Monday)

Hi Roberta

So pleased to hear you are okay for swimming and not suffering vertigo. I am not aware of any swimming pools on our journey tomorrow unless you would like to use our village pool to cool off when we get back in the afternoon ... not a very large pool or very deep ... it's more of an exercise pool rather than swimming.

I have provisionally earmarked Monday, 2nd April to go over to 'Straddie' and return on the Thursday morning before Good Friday ... so you would definitely need your cossie then. Still depends upon

Avis looking after the boys and you being free for those days ... talk about it tomorrow.

Take care, Martin

20 March, (Tuesday) – Drove to Martin's – he drove to Brisbane and showed me some sights near Wellington Point.

24 March (Friday) – Martin came to Gold Coast – we had dinner with Babette and Doug at the Italian restaurant.

29 March (Thursday) – I drove to Martin's. We attended Martin's friend Kevin's birthday party at the Leisure Centre. Stayed at Martin's overnight – drove home the next day.

Just before I left to spend the day at Martin's, a parcel arrived. In it were two copies of the Arabic (Lebanon) version of my Dealing with Difficult People book. Every time I receive a new version of my books, it's comparable to seeing a baby for the first time - I never know what they will look like!

30 March – (Friday) - I signed a contract with a Spanish publisher for my Dealing with School Bullying book. It will be released in September, 2008.

CHAPTER 3
APRIL - JULY, 2007

2 April – (Monday) - I drove to Martin's then he drove us over to Stradbroke Island ferry so we could spend a couple of days at Lorna's summer place. Martin showed me some of the lovely scenery and spectacular cliffs. He showed me where he had scattered his wife's ashes. We went back to Martin's the next day.

6 April, (Monday) I received an e-mail from a publisher in Greece asking whether they could publish my Dealing With Difficult People and Dealing with Difficult Situations – at Work and at Home books. I sent a reply saying I was interested in their offer.

8 April, (Sunday) – Martin came to dinner and stayed overnight.

18 April (Wednesday) – contract signed for me to present four days of seminars in May for a client in Singapore.

21 April, (Saturday) – Martin drove to Gold Coast. We had dinner with Babette and Doug at a nearby Italian restaurant.

26 April, (Friday) - I received an email stating that the Greek publisher would not be publishing my books.

26 April, (Friday) – I drove to Martin's – he helped prepare the Master Chef dinner at the Leisure Centre. I stayed for the weekend.

28 April (Sunday) - We met Lorna and John at a restaurant for breakfast.

Later that afternoon in conversation with Martin, I learned that he had to report to 'Mother' (the Meridien management group) any time I stayed overnight in his villa. I asked him if he had to report to her when he was not going to be home and he replied 'That's none of her business.' I replied 'Well me staying overnight at your place is none of her business either.'

He explained the management group insisted that if there was an emergency at the complex they needed to know how many people were there. My reply was, 'If you are at my place on the Gold Coast for the weekend, they wouldn't know and there must be hundreds of others that would not be home either. I said it was asinine that we had to act like school children and report in with our 'parents.'

MAY

4 May, (Friday) – Martin came to the Gold Coast and we enjoyed seeing the production 'Danny Bhoy at the Gold Coast Art Centre.

5 May, (Saturday) – We had a lovely dinner with friends Babette, Doug, Marny and Jeff at a Thai restaurant.

12 May, (Saturday) – I drove to Martin's to celebrate the 50th wedding dinner for his friends Barry and Wanita.

13 May, (Sunday morning) – Martin drove me to the Brisbane Airport. I flew to Singapore to present my seminars.

14 May, (Monday) – I presented my most popular one-day seminar entitled Dealing with Difficult People.

15 May, (Tuesday) – I was a keynote speaker at Singapore Women's conference.

16 May, (Wednesday) – I had a meeting with McGraw Hill in Singapore to discuss having them publish my Dealing with Difficult People book.

17 May, (Thursday) – I presented another Dealing with Difficult People session from 9:00 am till 4:00 pm.

18 May, (Friday) – I presented a one-day seminar for executive secretaries.

19 May, (Saturday) – I flew home to Brisbane. Martin met me at the airport and I spent the night at Martin's. We discussed the possibility of us going to Canada to travel through Western Canada, see my family and go on a cruise through the Inside Passage to Alaska. Martin was very keen – couldn't wait to go.

27 May, (Sunday) – We confirmed our flights and cruise to Canada and Alaska.

JUNE

14 June, (Thursday) – contract signed by Curtea Veche Romanian publisher for Dealing with Difficult People book.

16 June, (Saturday) – Martin here for dinner – Chinese food. He left the next day.

22 June, (Friday) – to Martin's – stayed the weekend.

29 June, (Friday) – paid for the Alaska cruise. I drove to Martin's for Master Chef dinner. It was a delightful meal.

30 June, (Saturday) – I had Babette, Doug and Martin for dinner at my place.

JULY

7 July, (Saturday) – Martin picked me up on the Gold Coast then we drove to his villa. Martin's friends gave us a bon voyage party at the Leisure centre. His friends Frank and Barry prepared the meal for us.

July 8, (Sunday) – We were driven to the airport to start our trip to Canada. Boarded the plane in Brisbane and flew to Taipei. We stayed overnight at the beautiful Jack Nicolas Golf and Country Club in Taipei.

9 July (Monday) – We flew from Taipei to Vancouver to Edmonton and spent our time visiting my relatives and friends.

16 July, (Monday) – Martin and I rented a car and set off for the 3,000 km trip through the Rocky Mountains to Kelowna to see my daughter and her family. Then we continued on to Calgary then Lethbridge where some friends of mine took us on a day trip that included viewing the Head Bashed In Buffalo Jump. The Indians used to set up their tepees at the base of the cliff and then drive the bison over the cliff to kill for their winter food. Many years later the bones were used for fertilizer and ammunition.

Next we drove to the area where on April 29th, 1903; the side of the mountain came down over the town of Frank killing 80 people - most of the people in the village. Several miners were trapped for four days, but escaped on their own. Another section of this mountain is expected to collapse at any time, but the people living there ignore that issue.

Next, our friends drove us over the US border. Because Martin was the only one who did not have a Canadian passport, he was fingerprinted and photographed. We saw more of the Rocky

Mountains; this time the US ones. We backtracked and drove through the Logan Pass and had lunch at Lake MacDonald where we took pictures of the cute resident gophers (called prairie dogs in Canada).

We returned to Lethbridge, then Martin and I drove to Drumheller which has a wonderful dinosaur museum – some of the bones go back six hundred million years and others only one hundred and fifty. There were hundreds of skeletons; one of the best displays in the world. We then drove back to Edmonton and looked forward to the last part of our trip – the cruise to Alaska.

I was very pleased that my friends and family had made Martin's first visit to Canada a truly special event.

29 July, (Sunday) - We flew again over the Rockies with Martin busy taking more photos. In Vancouver, we boarded the Norwegian Sun for a seven-day cruise through the inside passage of Alaska.

CHAPTER 4

AUGUST, SEPTEMBER and OCTOBER 2007

5 August, (Sunday) – We ended our cruise. We arrived in Vancouver at 8:00 am, took a taxi to the airport and caught our flight to Taipei. This time we did not stay overnight - had only a short wait until we caught our next flight to Brisbane.

7 August, (Tuesday) - Because of the time change we arrived back on 7 August. We were picked up at the airport and I stayed overnight at Martin's.

8 August, (Wednesday) – Martin drove me home and then he drove home to the village.

16 August, (Friday) – I drove to the village. That evening Martin and I went to Brisbane to see the production of Miss Saigon.

18 August, (Sunday) – Martin cooked and served at the Sunday Brekkie at the Leisure Centre. I drove home that afternoon.

Martin compiled a wonderful movie of our Canadian visit which included film, photos, voiceovers and music. It was very professionally done. Unfortunately, the Alaska cruise portion was not completed.

27 August, (Monday) – Martin came to the Gold Coast for my birthday – he had asked me what I needed – I told him I needed a set of carving knives because mine were very dull, so that's what he gave me. I received many other lovely gifts for my birthday. Because Babette, Doug and I are all Virgos, the four of us celebrated our birthdays at a restaurant that evening.

SEPTEMBER

8 September, (Saturday) – I drove to Martin's – stayed overnight.

9 September, (Sunday) – Martin drove me to the Brisbane Airport. I flew to Singapore to start presenting my seminars.

Several years before, I had contemplated retiring from presenting seminars, but when I considered the benefits I received when I did them – I decided to continue presenting them. When I presented seminars for overseas clients, they paid for all my travelling expenses (including meals) as well as a hefty daily fee for me to present my seminars. They had a limo ready at the airport when I arrived in Singapore and put me up in five star hotels. This visit, I stayed in the Singapore Hilton Hotel on the executive floor.

10 & 11 September, (Monday and Tuesday) – I conducted a 2-day Writing course.

12 September, (Wednesday) – I did a bit of shopping and had lunch with my friend Delphine Ang, a Singapore client of mine who would arrange public seminars and hire me to do the sessions. She had not hired me for this visit, but we had remained close friends.

13 September, (Thursday) – I presented a 1-day session called Time Control for Administrative Professionals.

14 September, (Friday) – I presented a 1-day session called Sharpening your skills as an executive/personal assistant.

15 & 16 September, (Saturday and Sunday) - I had the weekend off and did some sightseeing and shopping.

17 September, (Monday) – I presented a 1-day session called Creative Problem Solving.

18 September, (Tuesday) – I presented my most popular 1-day session called Dealing with Difficult People.

19 September, (Wednesday) – I flew back to Brisbane. Martin met me at the airport, took me to his home for brekkie then I drove home.

22 September, (Saturday) – Martin came and joined Liz and David Smith (my New Zealand friends) and me for dinner at my place.

28 September, (Friday) – Drove to Martin's for dinner – stayed the weekend.

OCTOBER

6 -25 October - I went on a nineteen-day trip that included two bus excursions and a fifteen-day river cruise down the Danube with my Canadian friend Agnes Fisher. I had planned this trip before I met Martin, so was sad to leave him for so long a time.

27 October (Saturday) – Martin and I had dinner at Liz and David's at their Gold Coast apartment.

28 October, (Monday) – I had to buy new battery for my car.

31 October, (Wednesday) – signed a new book contract with Alma Littera in Lithuania.

CHAPTER 5
NOVEMBER, 2007

3 November, (Saturday) - I was on the M1 (Pacific Highway) driving towards Martin's home when my car simply died. Thankfully I was able to manoeuvre my car over to the side of the road without incident. I was just looking for my RACQ information and was startled when I heard a tap on my window. It was a tow truck operator driving an RACQ vehicle. He had been travelling and saw that I was having difficulties. He drove me to their compound that was some distance from where Martin lived. He said it was the alternator that had gone and would need replacing. Because the shop was closed for the weekend, I had to leave the car there until it was fixed. Martin picked me up at the repair place and I stayed at Martin's till the car was fixed.

4 November (Sunday) – Martin and I went to a BBQ at noon and came back feeling quite mellow (from wine). Martin decided we should talk about our relationship and our future. He explained that he was tired of travelling back and forth as we had been doing for many months. He suggested that we live together, but that he was not keen on 'living in sin' as he called it. His second suggestion was that we get married. So I'd have to decide whether I wanted to take that step or just live together for a while. The difficulty was that if I lived in his villa, he had to get permission from the retirement village management. He also suggested that we have a joint ownership in the home (I would pay for half the value). This would be a major change for me and would involve many facets of my life. I asked him for time to think about it.

Martin explained that an alternative would be that he sell his unit in the retirement village and we buy another one together. However, this would involve a huge financial loss for him. I did not know that he would have to give 30% of the value of his property plus 50% of the capital gains he had accrued in the value of his home to Meridien if he sold his unit. This would mean he could lose between $200,000 to $250,000 if he sold his unit. This made me understand that there really was no option for us unless I moved in with him.

Because his unit had only a single car garage it could cause difficulties if I kept my car. I told him that I would not want to sell my car. He said he couldn't understand why I would need my own car and yet his daughter Lorna had objected to that same issue with her new partner. I explained that if I moved in with him, I would already have given up a lot of my independence and by giving up my car I would be completely dependent upon him. He suggested that I put the ownership of his car in my name. I felt that he didn't really understand the problem - but was sure he would change his mind. I asked if there was somewhere else I could park my car and he said he would look into it.

We learned that my car was fixed and ready to pick up, so Martin drove me over to collect it. We parted there and I drove back to the Gold Coast to think over our situation. I weighed the pros and cons of moving in with him and the balance swayed towards the benefits of doing so. There were some important cons, but if we worked on them, I thought we would be able to cohabit quite well together. We had got on fine for the month that we had been in Canada, not one disagreement, so that was a good sign.

5 November 6:11 pm (I emailed my Canadian friend Pat for advice.)

Hi Pat,

(I told her about the events that had occurred relating to Martin's and my relationship and the decisions I had to make then added the following):

I'm now home after paying $425 ransom for my car - needed a new alternator, battery boost and new fan belt. I'm still in a quandary regarding Martin. Here's what I've written down as being the situation:

1. His dining room could be my office (he suggested this).
2. His kitchen now has wicker chairs etc (that he calls his family room). I dislike wicker and think his dining room furniture would be best there. His comment 'I'd have to sell the family room furniture or give the existing table etc. to my daughter Lorna.' He was not fussy on having the dining room furniture in the 'family room.' (He has a living room that he calls his 'media room' where he has sound surround and plasma TV - still the living room as far as I am concerned - we wouldn't need a family room and a living room.

3. My bedroom – We both felt that we were both light sleepers, so would have our own bedrooms. I said I would want my own bed - he questioned this and commented, 'I'd have to sell the existing bed then.'
4. I would be expected to sell (I say put in storage) the remainder of my furniture except my bed and office stuff. He questioned why I would put it in storage - I said because I liked my furniture.
5. He has only a one car garage and driveway. He couldn't understand why I wanted my own car (doesn't understand that I would be living in 'his' house with 95% of the stuff his and that he also wanted me to lose my entire independence by giving up my car? I don't think so! Especially since he has a driveway. He says he will ask the management of the complex whether I could do this. This would be a crucial issue with me - I will NOT give up my car!
6. He suggested that I buy out half of his property and it be put in both our names. The property is worth about $500,000, but if it was sold would be worth less than $300,000 after the management team took their share of it.
7. The management group has to approve of me moving in! Boy do they have power over their residents! Don't know whether they would allow me to do so unless I was married to him. This too is a huge issue. I say he retain ownership (with it going to his daughter should he die) and I pay half of the expenses.
8. I see that there are three options: live together, marry, or continue as we are - he: two options - we marry or we continue as we are. He wants total commitment - I'm not ready for that and doubt if he understands that.

I think my next step is to suggest that he put himself in my shoes. Suppose he was going to move in with me and I would not let him bring in anything except a few of his personal belongings - would not allow him to have his car, and that I wanted him to buy half of my property (should I have owned one). It will be interesting to see what he would say.

This is all so new to me that I am reeling (as you can tell). Needed to vent on someone - glad you are there!

Cheers, Roberta

6 November [My email to Martin and his comments]

Hi Sweetie

I have spent a very restless night thinking about what we have discussed during the past two days. I was overwhelmed by your suggestion that we get married – I had contemplated that we might live together but had not really contemplated marriage.

I didn't actually get on me knees and propose!!! I was trying to get your feelings on the matter. These you have now made clear and I agree with you that we need to live together first ... and herein lies another 'negative problem ... what do we do if it doesn't work out?

The first thing I see needing resolution – is obtaining permission from the management group for me to move in. I would also need to know what their solution was for me parking my car there. I see these as crucial issues before we contemplate any changes.

I agree and I am still awaiting contact with Michelle.

When we discussed what you thought would be the best solution, I became more and more anxious because of the changes I anticipated *(don't anticipate ... I am fully aware that many major changes would need to be made in the layout and organisation of the villa)* I would need to make. To put our situation in perspective for you, let's say we were to reverse roles:

- You would leave your home and all your friends at the village and move into my home on the Gold Coast (let's say I owned my home).
- You would buy out half of my property, but only after the Management group of my complex approved of you and accepted you as a resident.
- You would have to sell your car because we only have a one-car garage.
- You would be able to bring the contents of your office and would be able to bring your own bed to sleep in. All the rest of your property you would either sell or put it into storage.

How would you react if these were your choices?

I have already considered them as fairly unworkable and have been thinking of a further alternative ... such as buying a property together and starting from scratch – despite the fact that I would lose some $200,000 from my capital due to the villa sale restrictions. My main concern is the safety of the boys and I would need to be able to construct a penned area in any new environment ... not possible in your present home!

What are my thoughts about us living together? Before I could consider a full commitment (marriage) I would need to know that we could live together comfortably. This would be accomplished by us living together (without marriage) until this was confirmed.

I agree.

To accomplish this, I suggest that I move some of my furniture etc. (including my office stuff) into your home and share expenses. This would be after my lease is up (I must give notice by the end of January).

That still leaves us a further three months for further discussions and we have only just opened the subject.

What are your thoughts about this? Or would you prefer to leave things as they are?

I gather that you would ... am I right? I have no strong feelings at this stage, but may have as I get older and less active. As it stands at the moment, we get on well together, meet fairly regularly and spend holidays together, whilst keeping full independence. The whole crux of the matter appears to evolve around you moving here and until I have had meaningful discussions with Meridien and then obtain your reaction to any restrictions they may apply, there are no decisions to be made. Having said that, my reason for raising the subject last weekend was because I realise that I do love you and as such would prefer to have your company every day and not just at weekends. Speak to you later. Love B.

7 November, (Wednesday) – The village celebrated their own version of Oktoberfest at Martin's. Before leaving for the event, we discussed the logistics of having me move in with him and discussed selling a bit of his furniture and using some of mine. I would be able to use his dining room for my office. We decided I would stay in my

rental unit until my lease ran out on February 11th which would give us both time to prepare for my moving in with him.

10 November, (Saturday) – Martin and I had dinner at Babette and Doug's home. I had spoken with my landlord (Shirley) and she said that rather than rent the townhouse out again, she would sell it. She asked me whether I could move out before the rental deadline if necessary – I said that it would be no problem.

17 November, (Saturday) – I drove to Martin's. We attended a live comedy show at a local theatre with some of Martin's friends.

23 November, (Friday) – I enjoyed the Master Chef Christmas dinner and happy hour at the village.

25 November, (Sunday) - Martin prepared and served at the Brekkie at the Leisure Centre. I drove back to the Gold Coast.

26 November, (Monday) - The first real estate group came to view my rental unit on the Gold Coast.

That day, I received a contract from a US publisher. My contract with Firefly Books had lapsed and I needed another publisher to take over distribution of my books. However, the contract they sent wasn't at all suitable. Their contract stated that they (the publisher) would retain the copyright for my book 'Dealing with Difficult Situations at Work' (they would not use the 'At Home' portion). They wanted all kinds of concessions. I sent them a contract that I would accept, knowing in my heart that they would not accept - so it was rather frustrating

I had a talk with Babette - they would like to have dinner with us next Saturday seeing we will not be on the Gold Coast for quite a few weekends.

26 November, 4:28 pm

Hi Roberta,

I have just received my Telstra Magazine and have attached the multiple (2nd phone number on the original line) for incoming calls. I was wondering if we could opt for items 1 &3 @ $6 per month. I would just need to have an extension put into the dining room for this to work and the 2nd number could be unique for your business. What do you think? Love, Martin

26 November, 5:30 pm

Hi Martin,

I think we could run into difficulties if the second line was for a business – we'd likely have to pay a business line rate. However, possibly the second line could be for your number and I could make it a business expense for both. We'd have to look into it. It's worth a call to them to see what they have to say.

By the way, the first real estate person (from L.J. Hooker) called – they'll bring someone down to have a look at the unit tomorrow about noon. Love, R.

27 November, (Tuesday) 12:18 pm

Hi Martin,

What a busy day it's been. L.J. Hooker brought in eight of their salespeople to see the place at 9:30 and four of them came back with prospective buyers at noon. They've just left. One of the couples are definitely going to put a bid on the property and mid to the end of February would be great for possession. They do have to sell their own home first though. I'll keep you informed. Cheers, R.

28 November, (Wednesday) 10:47 am

Hi Roberta,

I have submitted a request for a 2nd telephone line to be installed into the dining room. Love, M.

Hi Sweetie,

You're too good to me!

Thanks for doing that. Will the line be registered to Cava Consulting? Whatever it costs you to install it let me know and I will reimburse you for it. Love, R.

27 November 3:03 pm

Hi Sweetie pie,

Looks as if you are in for a turbulent few days until a contract is signed.

Michelle Smith has just been on the phone to say that we are being sent a licence form from Meridien's solicitors in a week, or so, for signature by both of us and return. Also to contact her immediately if there is something we do not understand or agree with. She has also told me to contact the village Manager, Diane, to have a second phone line installed and to contact Kath (sales) for a personalised parking spot. So things are now moving at this end!!

I am busy trying to print cards, annual Christmas letter and further copies of our holiday disc to send to the UK, plus calendars to some of them.

Bye for now, Love, M.

27 November – we confirmed our trip to New Zealand where we would stay with my friends Liz and David Smith then tour the South Island. Leave January 19th – return February 2nd.

28 November, (Wednesday)

Good Morning,

I have had my home contents insurance renewal from Suncorp and wondered if I should add anything of yours to it? I have contents cover for $77,000 - new for old - with an annual premium of around $460. The house is covered on the owners insurance.

The premium is due before 21st December so there is plenty of time to discuss. I think all I might need to do is add your name and office equipment plus stock of books???? Give it some thought.

Love, Martin

28 November

Hi yourself!

You would have to check to see whether office equipment has a ceiling (as far as value). All my stuff is insured for $57,000 that includes office stuff. However much of that will go into storage and I will have to insure it separately. I think there is a limit as to how much you can ask for computer equipment unless you have a business insurance policy. With us both having two computers it does complicate things. Might be worthwhile to check that out with your insurer. I have mine with APIA (the special insurance company for retirees who might work a bit).

I would say my office stuff plus supply of books/workbooks would have to be insured for about $25,000. My policy runs until 29 May, 2008.

See what you can find out ... Love, R.

CHAPTER 6
DECEMBER, 2007

1 December (Saturday) - Martin came for dinner with Babette and Doug at the Thai restaurant.

2 December, (Sunday) am

Hi Martin,

I was going through some stuff to give to St. Vincent's and wonder if the Village can use seven white coffee mugs I was going to give away. They are almost new, and I was quite sure they had white dishes.

Please let me know.

By the way, a young couple came through today with the real estate agent - she is expecting her first baby about New Years' Eve and they have just decided that they want to have their own home before it's born!!! Dah - that's less than one month away people!

They are very serious about the place and are likely going to put an offer in for it today with possession before the end of December. It'll be interesting to see what happens - probably nothing!

However, it has urged me to go through even more stuff to see what I can give away etc. Cheers, R.

3 & 4 December (Monday and Tuesday) – More people came to see the unit.

6 December, (Thursday) 8:51 am

Hi Roberta,

Angela has just said 'yes please' for the mugs. They would be very handy in the coffee shop.

We had some heavy rain around 3 o'clock yesterday, but not as much as the Gold Coast. I bet Springbrook falls are cascading well at the moment ... still got an Alaska hat to reclaim from up there!!

Love, M.

PS It had to happen!!!......I have lost a hearing aid!!!

7 December, (Friday) – I signed a contract for my book: 'How Women Can Advance in Business' with the Kenya publisher.

8 December, (Saturday) – dinner with Martin's neighbours.

12 December (Wednesday) – Retirement Village Christmas dinner at Leisure Centre. Martin and I had opened a joint bank account and both deposited $1,000 into it. We also opened a joint MasterCard account we could use for home expenses.

15 December, (Saturday) – we celebrated Martin's 73rd birthday.

17 December, (Monday)

Martin sent me a copy of the letter he received from Michelle Smith along with a copy of the Long Term Guest Licence:

17 December 2007 *[1]

BY COURIER

Mr Martin Williams & Ms Roberta Cava
(Martin's address)

Dear Mr Williams & Ms Cava,

Long Term Guest Licence

Please find **enclosed** the Long Term Guest Licence pertaining to Villa 3196 Wellington Manor Retirement Village (in duplicate).

Could you please sign both copies of the Licence, where indicated, and return to my attention. Upon receipt of same, we shall also execute the Licence and then return one (1) original to you for safekeeping.

As previously advised, we strongly encourage you to seek independent legal and/or financial advice before signing the enclosed.

If you have any queries in relation to this matter, please do not hesitate to contact me.

Yours sincerely,

Wellington Manor Pty Ltd
Michelle Smith
General Manager, Queensland

LONG TERM GUEST LICENCE *[2]

THIS DEED made the _____ day of _____ 2007

BETWEEN: **WELLINGTON MANOR PTY LTD ACN 054 667 024** of Level 16, Waterfront Place, 1 Eagle Street, Brisbane in the state of Queensland ('The Operator')

AND: **ROBERTA CAVA** of Villa 3196, Wellington Manor, Wellington Point in the state of Queensland ('the Guest')

AND **MARTIN JOSEPH WILLIAMS** of Villa 3196, Wellington Manor, Wellington Point in the state of Queensland ('the Resident')

RECITALS:

A The Resident is the lessee under registered lease no. 705068890 between the Resident and the Operator dated 30 August 2001 ('the Lease').

B. Pursuant to the Lease, the Resident has the right to reside in Villa 3196 in 'Wellington Manor Retirement Village,' Wellington Point, Queensland ('the Village') as that villa is described in the Lease ('the Unit'). The Operator is the registered owner of the land in which the Unit is located and operates the village.

C. The parties agree to allow the Guest to reside in the unit with the Resident on the terms contained in this licence.

TERMS:

1. **GRANT OF LICENCE**

The operator grants to the Guest a licence to reside in the Unit jointly with the Resident on the terms contained in this licence.

2. **TERM**

(a) The Licence commences on the date of this Licence.

(b) The Licence expires on the sooner of:

   (i) The death of the Guest; or

   (ii) The date that the Guest is required to vacate the Unit in accordance with Clause 4 of this Licence.

3. **OCCUPATION OF UNIT**

(a) The Guest:

   (i) acknowledges that it occupies the Unit and resides within the Village entire at its own risk;

(ii) releases the Operator from all liability (whether in contract, tort, by statute or otherwise however) in respect of all claims whatever relating to the use and occupation of the Unit by the Guest and the residing within the Village by the Guest:

(iii) agrees to comply with and observe all the terms of the Lease (including any amendments to the same) during the term of the Lease and during any term that the Guest occupies the Unit under this Licence (including any time in occupation following the death of or vacation of the Unit by the Resident if applicable);

(iv) agrees to vacate the Unit on the date that the Guest is required to vacate pursuant to Clause 4: and

(v) agrees to pay all payments and outgoings under the Lease including, but not limited to, any general service charges, maintenance reserve fund contributions or personal services charges during the term of the Licence (including any term in occupation of the Unit following the death of or vacation of the Unit by the Resident if applicable).

(b) The Resident acknowledges that:

(i) Where following the death of or the vacation of the Unit by the Resident the Guest remains in occupation of the Unit, the Operator is under no obligation to locate a new resident for the Unit until the Guest vacates the Unit or where a date for the Guest to vacate the Unit pursuant to the terms of this Licence has been determined. Accordingly, the payment and calculation of the exit fee and exit entitlement (as those terms are defined in the Lease) and any other entitlements or payments under the lease payable on termination of the Lease may be postponed if the Guest elects to occupy the Unit (subject to the terms of this Licence) following the death or vacation of the Unit by the Resident; and

(ii) the Guest may occupy the Unit following the death of the Resident (in accordance with Clause 4 of this Licence) which occupation may impact on the cost (i.e. by increasing the works and the costs of such works) relating to the reinstatement work (as that term is defined in the Lease).

4. **TERMINATION OF THE LICENCE**

(a) The Guest may terminate this Licence at any time during the term of this Licence by giving the Operator thirty (30) days prior written notice of their intention to terminate this Licence and vacate the Unit.

(b) The Operator may terminate this Licence:

   (i) If the Guest is in default of this Licence – by giving the Guest at least thirty (30) days written notice that this Licence is terminated and the Guest is required to vacate the Unit;

   (ii) If the Resident dies or vacates the Unit ('in this clause, collectively referred to as the 'Resident Leave Date'), and the Guest has prior to the Resident Leave Date occupied the Unit pursuant to this Licence for more than six (6) months, and the Guest is occupying the Unit at the Resident Leave Date – by the Operator giving the Guest at least three (3) months written notice that this Licence is terminated and the Guest is required to vacate the Unit;

   (iii) If the Resident dies or vacates the Unit, ('in this clause, collectively referred to as the Resident Leave Date'), and the Guest has prior to the Resident Leave Date occupied the Unit pursuant to this Licence for less than six (6) months, and the Guest is occupying the Unit at the Resident Leave Date – by the Operator giving the Guest at least thirty (30) days written notice that this Licence is terminated and the Guest is required to vacate the Unit; or

   (iv) If the Lease is terminated by the Operator pursuant to the provisions of the Lease – by the Operator giving to the Guest the same notice required to be given to the Resident under the terms of the Lease to vacate the Unit.

5. **GUEST TO INDEMNIFY OPERATOR**

The Guest releases and indemnifies the Operator and agrees to keep the Operator and its employees, agents and contractors released and at all times indemnified to the fullest extent permitted by law from and against all claims of every description whatever incurred by the Operator or for which the Operator may be or become liable whether in contract, tort, by statute or otherwise however and whether during or after the term of the Licence in respect of or arising from, the use and occupation of the Unit by the Guest and the residing in the Village by the Guest.

6. COVENANT

This Licence is personal to the Guest and is not assignable to any other person or entity.

7. GUEST'S RIGHT OF OCCUPATION

The Guest has a personal right of occupation of the Unit on the terms contained in this Licence and has no legal interest in the land on which the Unit is situated on or the Unit or any right to exclusive possession of the Unit. The Guest acknowledges that they are not a 'resident' as that term is defined under the Retirement Villages Act 1999 (as amended from time to time).

8. COSTS AND STAMP DUTY

(a) The Guest shall bear their own costs of and incidental to the preparation, execution and stamping of this Licence and any ancillary documentation relating to the Licence and all stamp duty payable on this Licence.

(b) The Resident will pay the Operators costs of and incidental to the preparation and execution of this Licence and any ancillary documentation relating to the Licence.

IN WITNESS OF THE SAME this Deed has been duly executed.

EXECUTED BY WELLINGTON MANOR RETIREMENT VILLAGE PTY LTD ACN 054 667 024 as the Operator this _____ day of _____ 2007 in accordance with the Corporations Act:

_____

Director

_____

Director

SIGNED SEALED AND DELIVERED by **ROBERTA CAVA** as the Guest this _____ day of _____ 2007 in the presence of:

_____

A Justice of the Peace/Solicitor

SIGNED SEALED AND DELIVERED by **MARTIN JOSEPH WILLIAMS** as the Guest this _____ day of _____ 2007 in the presence of:

_____

17 December, (Monday) 1:29 pm

Hi Martin,

I forgot to mention that the Romanian publisher I found on the internet is one that has signed an agreement directly with me. They had an earlier contract that lapsed in April of this year. I didn't think their version would be out till 2008 - so they moved fast.

Cheers, R.

17 December, 4:11 pm

Hi Martin,

It's confirmed - the people will be moving into my place on Feb 14th, so I think I will arrange for movers for Feb 11th (the same day my phone is to be hooked up at your place).

Now I will have to make arrangements with Ozemail. How should we do that - from your end as part of your broadband connection - or do I have to do it from this end? We will require far more download capabilities, so it might cost more than you are paying now, but less than if I had my own account. Love, R.

17 December, 5:48 pm

Good news that you now have a moving date ... I have the computer man coming on Wednesday morning to connect up the new High speed ADSL so I will ask him about the best way to add your email address. I have already upgraded my subscription for larger downloads so will check out if it is enough. Love, M.

Hi Roberta,

This is what you sent to me. I believe we only need to take a copy to the Lawyer and let him include it in a letter to Meridien requesting clarification/changes to the document. I doubt he will be able to do it during our first visit because there is too much background (PID) for him to become familiar with before responding, unless he gets onto Michelle by phone whilst we are there, but I doubt he will accept verbal responses, given her track record to date!!?

I will have to forego a massage this Wednesday as I have to be back here by five for an executive committee meeting prior to next Tuesday's meeting of the full committee.

Will send you a copy of the Cohab agreement complete with my comments later. Love, M.

18 December

Hi Sweetheart,

Michelle is in Melbourne today and back in her office tomorrow morning, so no answer on my questions until then. Although Dianne rang to say that she is arranging for an extra front gate remote for your car ... at a cost of course because there is normally only one remote for each villa ... even Spencer only has one with his double garage!! Dianne also said that they are in the process of marking out three designated parking places of which you will have one.

I am out to the men's club Xmas get together (drinks and nibbles) at 5pm with Brian followed by pool at Pam. Got my UK bank fixed last night and hope to get my office outlook fixed tomorrow. Have also booked the boys for their annual vaccinations on 7th January so they will be 'in date' for the cattery. I have also (did I tell you?) booked the Lake Hawea Motel, so our NZ accommodation is now fully booked. I have also booked the coach, cruise, fly back (weather permitting) to Milford Sound and this day out will be at my expense. Temperature in NZ at the moment is 30 degrees, so I don't know how Liz is coping with her 'cooler' summer?? Love, Martin

17 December, 3:34 pm (After we'd had dinner with his daughter and her partner, John.)

Hi Martin,

Here are two pictures - one of us and one of Lorna and John (I think theirs is great!) Cheers, R

17 December, 4:41pm

Hi Roberta,

Did you send one to Lorna? If not, I am sure she will love it.

Storms on the way so may not be able to play bowls this evening.

Michelle has rung to say the 'licence' will be couriered to me tomorrow!!! Cheers, M

17 December, 4:41 pm

Hi Martin,

Yes, I did send the same pictures to Lorna. One of us as well.

That's good the 'licence' is coming. We will have to decide when to make the appointment with the lawyer. Cheers, R.

18 December, (Tuesday) 5:41pm

Hi Martin,

I've received the credit card that is ours (my name only) - but only one card - wonder if they will send another in your name?? I may have to ask for one (but I thought the gal was going to look after that). There's a form in the package about obtaining a second card. They have sent the pin number for it addressed to both of us, so don't know whether you will have a card in your name or whether it will be in my name. Will wait to see what they send next.

Glad about your personal credit card and that it will be good for a few years. I wonder if that's because you will soon be 'attached' to an Aussie citizen?

What is the cost of the front gate remote?

I have obtained an estimate of what it will cost me to move - approximately $1,150. The fellow says that I will not likely need so much space to store my stuff so it shouldn't be over $200 per month. I'll have to wait till I get closer to the time of moving to see exactly what will be going into storage.

By the way, it's David that can't stand the heat - Liz doesn't mind at all - she didn't want to go back to NZ - it was entirely David's idea.

Love, R.

18 December, (Tuesday)

Dear Michelle,

Thank you for sending me the Long Term Guest Licence by courier and for your messages on my answer phone. I must say I was surprised that the document had less pages than the Parking Licence ... I was expecting a mini PID!! However, it all seems fairly clear and succinct to present to our lawyer.

Before I take it down to Roberta at Varsity Lakes, I would like to clear up a couple of items that do not appear in the document but were covered, I believe, during our preliminary discussions.

Clause 4 - Termination of the Licence. I understood that in the event of my demise, Roberta would have the option to purchase the villa with the residue of monies going to my estate. This option is not listed but there is a statement at the top of page -2- The Resident acknowledges that: (i) which seems to be in conflict with the statements in clause 4(b)

Clause 7 - Guest's Right of Occupation. There is no mention of the 'Guest' having full right of access to the use of the village facilities. I understood that Roberta would be treated as a 'resident' to all intents and purposes for the issue of Leisure Centre and perimeter gate keys, plus a magic button remote for operating the front gates. Is this correct?

Would you please note that the provisional date for Roberta to commence living in the village is 11th February 2008.

Would you please call me to clarify the above points.

Kind regards

Martin

18 December

Hi Sweetie,

I just measured the space that my book display needs - it is just a tad under 42".

There was a program on TV (Channel 7) that was talking about all the illegal people that are getting into Australia. Might be a good time to tell them your story about having to wait so long for residency?

I'm wondering if you will be too busy with Ruth gone to come this Saturday. I will, after all, be coming to your place on Monday. Let me know if you are too busy to come.

Love, R.

19 December, (Wednesday)

Hi Martin,

I will comment through your email:

Good Morning sweetheart,

The book display would just fit under the kitchen top with about quarter of an inch to spare, but it might also look very good on the angled wall leading into your office so, either way, you should bring it. Will do.

I could do without coming down this weekend as there are still lots of things to do preparing the courtyard for Boxing Day, tables and chairs from the centre and working with the social committee for our Australia Day submission to the local council. We have won first prize for the last six years, so it would be nice to keep our record going ... our theme this year is 'Indigenous Animals Games'. However, I did promise to come down and also love being with you, so it may be a case of late arrival - early leave!!

I think you should not come so you're able to do the things you need to do without having to rush. I will be seeing you on Monday anyway, so that's just two days from then.

Re channel 7 - if I made waves I would probably alienate the immigration people and go to the back of the queue. Love, M.

I had a wonderful surprise when I opened my mail yesterday - it was an email from that lovely New Zealand policeman I told you about that was so kind to me when I lost my passport. He is now living on the Sunshine Coast (Sippy Downs - on the way to Mooloolaba) has left the police force, and he and his wife (and two teen-aged daughters) own a restaurant called 'Fried Green Tomatoes.'

I also got a letter from a large international architectural firm in Edmonton, Alberta asking about my seminars. They have offices in Edmonton, Toronto and in the USA. I've replied to their request for course outlines.

Got a bunch of boxes yesterday, so will slowly but surely fill them with stuff I will be storing. In the past, I have emptied out my filing cabinets, but wonder if that's necessary with them having a dolly to move them. I'll have to check before I start unloading them.

Have a good day, Love, Roberta

19 December, (Wednesday) 3:40 pm

Hi Martin,

By the way, I checked the phone in my kitchen - I will need two power plugs for my phone stuff alone, so wonder if we need four power plugs along the wall backing onto the kitchen rather than just two (cause that's where all my computer junk will be plugged in)??

Tomorrow (12:30 pm) L.J. Hooker has made arrangements to have the engineering and pest inspection of my rental unit.

I was able to get a bathroom set (glass, soap dispenser and toothbrush holder) at Spotlight the other day.

Thanks for looking into that letter that came to your post office.

Love, Roberta

20 December, 9:23 am

Hi Roberta,

Here is the relevant section of the Act that allows a relative (partner) the 1st option to purchase when the 'resident vacates the dwelling.' It seems to cover my query okay and I will attach a copy to the Long Term Licence for when we see a Lawyer. Love, M.

Dear Martin, *3

As discussed yesterday, please find attached an extract of the Retirement Villages Act 1999 - i.e. Section 70B, which deals with a relative's right to reside.

55 Right to reside in a retirement village terminates automatically on resident's death

> A right to reside in an accommodation unit in a retirement village held by a resident terminates on the death of the resident.

If your solicitor has any queries, please advise him that he may contact me.

Also, please note that my new mobile telephone number is (gave number)

Regards,

Michelle Smith
General Manager, Queensland

20 December, (Thursday) 11:10 am

Hi Martin,

Thanks for sending the page about Relative's right to reside.

Is the contract I'm expected to sign as a 'guest' called a residence contract?

It appears that the 'relative' can only stay in the residence for 3 months. It also seems that the 'relative' must buy the property (6) - in other words the management people would keep the $200,000+ and Lorna would get the rest. Then I would have to re-buy the property at the going rate (full price). Doesn't sound like much of a deal to me ... all slanted in their favour.

I've learned NOT to accept a verbal explanation (especially by lawyers). This section does not mention at any time what would happen should the person be a 'partner' rather than a 'relative.' They might need to add a clause to this that refers to me as a 'partner' rather than a 'relative.'

Thanks for sending me this information. Love, R.

22 December, (Saturday) 11:47 am

Hi Sweetheart,

Have just been sent a creed I can relate to ... thought you might need to know what you are tying up alongside!!!!

What time are you arriving on Monday and do you have your key with you? I have to collect the turkey and then take Roger to the vet hospital at Manly (my vet on holiday) at 11.45, so might not be in if you arrive before 1am.

I have ordered the voice operated text software, so hope it works okay. Love, M.

22 December, Saturday) 12:20 pm

Hi Martin,

You asked whether I was arriving before 1 am on Monday - no - I don't think so ... However I can arrive after 1:00 pm. if that's okay. Is Roger ill or is this just for a checkup? Yes, I have my key so no problem getting in.

I thought that voice operated program might be what you need so you can do documents quicker. The only problem might be that it is a US program and is likely programmed to respond to someone with a North American accent. I would ask them. I'd do fine with it wouldn't I? Love, R

22 December, 1:01 pm

Roger has a weeping sore on his chin and I think it is related to the pink patch on his nose. Kona has twice had this type of complaint and it required antibiotics to clear it up. Anyway, I can't let him suffer until my vet starts up on the 7th Jan.

The voice operated program is supposed to work in any country and language and has world-wide sales, so it should be okay. Love, Martin

22 December, 3:43 pm

Hi Martin,

I got a sad message from Canadian friends of mine - Pat Todd. Her husband, Norm is dying of cancer. I'm feeling very down after reading it - too many of my friends are dying of cancer these days.

Love, R.

22 December, 4:24 pm

Hi Roberta,

Such sad news when the end is near, just a general realisation that a fight for life is coming to an end ... the longer the fight, the harder the acceptance. One can only pray for a happy release from pain and then life goes on for those left behind until the next friend, or relative, is struck down by the dreaded C. One has to be selfish and be thankful for good health. I pray that we have many years of health and enjoyment left. Love, Martin

22 December, 4:57 pm

I'll drink to that ... Love, R.

24 December, (Monday) – Went to Martin's.

25 December (Tuesday) – Martin and I had lunch with his daughter Lorna and partner John.

26 December (Wednesday) - Christmas dinner at Martin's. His friend Frank cooked a huge turkey on the Webber for fourteen people. Babette and Doug drove up for the event and spent the night in Martin's spare bedroom.

27 December, (Thursday) – I drove back to the Gold Coast.

27 December, 3:50 pm

Hi Martin,

I've gone over the Meridien Long Term Guest Licence agreement and note the following:

3. (a) (ii) releases the Operator from all liability (whether in contract, tort, by statute or otherwise however) in respect of all claims whatever relating to, the use and occupation of the Unit by the Guest and the residing within the Village by the Guest;

Does this mean that if I'm injured on their common property they are absolved of all risk? (Such as being hit by flying branches etc that are being cut by maintenance workers?) If so – this is illegal. They have a duty of care for **anyone** coming on their property.

Are you covered by them if there's some kind of accident or injury that occurs on common property?

(This type of thing is repeated in clause #5 – which is also illegal and should be removed.)

5. **GUEST TO INDEMNIFY OPERATOR'**

The Guest releases and indemnifies the Operator and agrees to keep the Operator and its employees, agents and contractors released and at all times indemnified to the fullest extent permitted by law from and against all claims of every description whatever occurred by the Operator or for which the Operator may be or become liable whether in contract, tort, by statute or otherwise however and whether during or after the term of the Licence in respect of or arising from, the use and occupation of the Unit by the Guest and the residing in the Village by the Guest.

3. (a) (v) They have not identified why I would be responsible for these fees - general services charges, maintenance reserve fund etc. Why would I be responsible for those charges? I could see it if I was occupying the property after the 'resident' vacates the premises, but not if you are there. Did they explain this to you?

4. If you 'vacated' the premises before I was a 'guest' for 6 months - they could turf me out in 30 days - kinda scary! After 6 months it would be 3 months.

8. (a) There has been no mention to date of 'stamp duty' fees - did they mention this to you? And why would a person have to pay those fees anyway? Doesn't make sense why I would have to pay any stamp duty fees - they only apply to someone buying a property - I'm not doing that.

8. (b) will pay the Operators costs ... I would like the word 'reasonable' put into this agreement and they should have to prove why it is so expensive to prepare a 3-page standard document ($700.00).

As you mentioned, there is no mention about me having the full rights to use the facilities etc of the complex. These should be clearly defined so there is no question about what is and is not allowed.

Well - those are my observations. I will be so glad when this is over!!! I hate people who are greedy vultures - and Meridien are greedy vultures! Love, R.

28 December, 12:13 pm

Hi Martin,

I was going to send you the cohabitation agreement, but see that the USB disk that it was on is in the bag with my portable computer (it's in my bedroom at your place). There will be a couple of things I will change on the inventory list, so please send ME a copy after you have added your inventory so I have a copy here. Thanks,

It seems that everyone had a good time on Boxing Day - I know I did - but you were so busy I doubt if you did yourself. Next year hopefully you will let me help or even be in charge. Love, R.

28 December

Hi Roberta,

Yes I did enjoy Boxing Day and I know that everyone at the meal did too, but was a bit pooped afterwards when I wound down!!

The crockery is now in the drawer and I have cleared the second drawer (below) to ensure there is enough space for your stuff.

I am boiling the turkey carcass with left-over meat on it but haven't a clue how long to simmer it or what to do next? Presume I have to strain it after a couple of hours and save the stock?

I will send a copy of the cohabitation agreement later... am on bar duty this evening so must go down and prepare soon. Love M

28 December, 6:15 pm

Hi Martin,

Re: turkey

After you have boiled it for a while to loosen the meat from the bones and get the flavour into the stock - strain through a big strainer - then take all the meat off the bones - cut into small pieces and put back in the stock. Add whatever veggies and seasoning you want and enjoy! I usually add a bit of turkey stuffing - but Amelia's stuffing is much different to mine, so don't know whether that will work or not. Love, R.

29 December, (Saturday)

Hi Sweetheart,

Hope all is well with you. I seem to have loads of unfinished tasks and must now leave them to clean out the fish tank!! Miss you. Love Martin

29 December

Hi Martin,

Thanks for sending the cohabitation agreement - I now have a copy and have adjusted it accordingly.

I've booked my moving men. I had contacted Caloundra movers who moved me twice already, but they suggested I use MiniMovers. I looked them up and they are about the same price as them all but an added bonus is that they manage the National Storage in Capalaba, so know where it is and how it works. National Storage is booked too, but I have to go down there and sign some papers the next time I'm there on a business day.

Did I tell you that I've bought a new domain name - so now have two ways to attract people to my websites. This one is called: www.dealingwithdifficultpeople.info

I have just downloaded all my files; now will have to make sure Nick (my host guy) gets it on-line. I hope to sell a few books through that one. The domain itself only cost $24 for 2 years, and

Nick's contract states that he will look after two domain names for the price I was paying for one - so I had nothing to lose. I'll let you know when it's fully operational.

I've been busy taking my display cabinet down from the wall and putting everything in boxes. I'll bring it with me this time along with a few other boxes.

I miss you too - will be there on Monday. Love, R

31 December, (Monday) 7:12 am

Hi Martin,

Norm Todd passed away on December 29th - his birthday. I knew it was coming, but it's very sad to learn of his passing. Love, R.

31 December, 7:37 am

Hi Roberta,

Sorry to hear the sad news .It's always difficult for those left behind to come to terms. I will give you a consolation hug when you arrive today. Love, M

31 December

I spent New Year's Eve at the village with Martin at the Leisure Centre. Wore my slinky red dress and danced the night away (Martin is a great dancer). We had a great evening. Martin was MC.

CHAPTER 7

JANUARY, 2008

5 January, 2008, (Saturday)

Hi Martin,

The lake in front of my rental unit has flooded. So far it has covered the boat dock except for about 1 metre and is up to the stairs on the other side of the lake. Hopefully it will stop raining and the lake will drain into the ocean.

Don't forget to bring my glasses! Love, Roberta

5 January, (Saturday) Martin drove to the Gold Coast. We went to Burleigh Bowls Club with Babette Davidson and Doug Henderson. Had a lovely evening.

7 January, (Monday) 9:56 am

Hi Martin,

I've made an appointment with the lawyer about our Cohabitation Agreement and the Meridian paperwork for Wednesday, January 9th at 11:00 am.

Please confirm that this is okay. Love, R.

7 January, 10:45 am

Hi Roberta,

No problem. I will be with you around 10.00 am but will have to return the same day as I have an early appointment on Thursday. I will collect all the paperwork together, including the original PID I signed.

Have just returned from having the boys' annual vaccination, so will get onto the paperwork now.

By the way, Roger likes lying on the new rug!!! I tried putting up that blue curtain remnant but it was 6' short and did not look right, so I took it down. May try again when your blue sofa is in. Love, M.

7 January, 1:23 pm

Hi Martin,

Glad you can make it. Will you have time to put together a list of the questions I wanted to ask Meridien?

Do you want me to see if Sue can give you a massage on Wednesday afternoon or early evening?

See you Wednesday morning. Love, R.

January 7

Hi Sweetheart,

I have completed my draft for the cohab agreement and added in a reference to the Last Will and Testament. The paragraph numbering did not seem correct but no doubt the Lawyer will recommend changes and layout. I have also updated the title to avoid confusion.

I have contacted the electrician for extra power point and he reckons there could be a problem putting them on an internal wall, so it looks as if it will have to be installed on the outside wall to the left of the hatchway (viewing from inside the dining room.) He hopes to give me a date for later this week or early next week.

My voice is going with the sore throat; despite getting some linctus from the pharmacy ... you might have to do all of the talking on Wednesday!!!!

Not feeling too good so will go to bed with a hot toddy?? Love, M.

8 January, (Tuesday)

Hi Martin,

Sorry you are still feeling crook. Hopefully the hot toddy helped!

Thanks for sending the agreement. I have made the changes to my section so it should be ready to take with us tomorrow. Do you want me to make a copy of the final one for you to refer to? I will make one for the lawyer as well. Love, R.

January 8

Hi Roberta,

That sounds a good idea to have a final draft each ... did you note I forgot to mention the cats!!!

Still not feeling too good so will probably cancel the chiropractor this afternoon as the cough mixture makes one drowsy when driving, so will not be able to take any tomorrow before driving down to you, but I should be okay after a good night's sleep. Is the Lawyer far from you and what time do I need to be with you?

Kona is very quiet today from a reaction to the vaccination yesterday. It is normally Roger who gets the reaction, but he is full of beans.

Paula is here cleaning at the moment and was surprised at all the changes.

Cheers for now. Love, M.

8 January

Hi Martin,

I have made three copies of the agreement. Our appointment is for 11:00 am and it is just on the Gold Coast Highway in Mermaid, so will only take us about 15 minutes to get there.

It's hot as Hades here today and I've been busy packing and moving boxes. Will need a second shower soon! Love, R.

8 January

I am feeling a bit better as the throat has eased but I am now in the grips of a cold with sneezes and runny nose ... hopefully it will dry up a bit by tomorrow.

It was a good job I did go to the chiropractor because I had put my pelvis out again and had to have some hard bumps to put it back in alignment. He didn't think it was the NYE dancing ... more likely my dragging the furniture around was the root cause. I will be glad when you are in and we can get settled!!!!!

Time for dinner and six o'clock news. Love, Martin

9 January, (Wednesday) – Martin and I met with Michael Wright the lawyer about the Guest Licence, our cohabitation agreement and the Parking Agreement. Michael asked us who had prepared the Long Term Guest Licence. There were so many errors and omissions in it that he suggested it had been thrown together by a legal clerk – certainly not by a qualified lawyer. He advised that any agreement

signed by a resident, guest and owners was in fact a contract, not a licence to allow relatives, carers etc. to move into the retirement village and be free to use the village facilities. He advised us to remove two clauses because they absolved the Operators of their 'Duty of Care' responsibilities:

'Releases the Operator from all liability (whether in contract, tort, by statute or otherwise however) in respect of all claims whatever relating to the use and occupation of the Unit by the Guest and the residing within the Village by the Guest.' and,

'The Guest releases and indemnifies the Operator and agrees to keep the Operator and its employees, agents and contractors released and at all times indemnified to the fullest extent permitted by law from and against all claims of every description whatever incurred by the Operator or for which the Operator may be or become liable whether in contract, tort, by statute or otherwise however and whether during or after the term of the Licence in respect of or arising from, the use and occupation of the Unit by the Guest and the residing in the Village by the Guest.'

The lawyer also advised that there was nothing in the contract protecting Martin, if our relationship broke up, so he added a new item:

'The licence expires on the termination of the relationship of the guest and the resident.'

He also advised that because the licence was a template for many similar situations, there should be no charge to the resident. He also question the legal fee of $700 for a standard legal document that likely took about fifteen minutes to prepare (meaning the '*lawyer*' would be earning approximately $2,800 per hour). In fact, because the document had to be re-written, he advised us that we should not be paying **any** legal fee charged by the Operator.

He also cautioned that the clause stating to the following was very harsh and would be extremely stressful for a guest to have to vacate the premises so soon after the death of a partner:

'If the Resident dies or vacates the Unit, ('in this clause, collectively referred to as the Resident Leave Date'), and the Guest has prior to the Resident Leave Date occupied the Unit pursuant to this Licence for less than six (6) months, and the Guest is occupying the Unit at

the Resident Leave Date – by the Operator giving the Guest at least thirty (30) days written notice that this Licence is terminated and the Guest is required to vacate the Unit; '9 January, (Wednesday) - That evening after seeing our lawyer:

Hi Martin,

I have almost finished the Guest Licence and was going to duplicate one clause that was on the parking licence. However, you must have put that agreement into your case so I can't refer to it (you have the only copy). I think it was clause 5.1 and should be added to the RISK portion of the Guest licence.

Could you please type in the information that is in that section? Thanks.

Get well soon, Love, R.

9 January, (Wednesday) 5:35 pm

Hi Roberta,

The full section reads:

RISK

(a) The Licensee accepts that enjoyment of its (her) rights under this License are solely at is risk and indemnifies and releases Wellington Manor from any liability to any person (including other licensees and owners of cars and other motor vehicles) in any way connected with the use by the Licensee of the Car Parking Area, including:-

(i) personal injury or death of any person;

(ii) destruction theft of or damage to any property of any person including Cars and their contents.

(I believe this is the paragraph Michael was referring to) except where the loss (or death)??? was caused or contributed to by the negligent acts or omissions of Wellington Manor, its servants, agents, contractors or sub-contractors.

Is this what you wanted?)

Still feeling terrible so will go back to bed after some nourishing soup!!

Thanks for arranging the meeting today. I will attempt to arrange a meeting with Michelle tomorrow for a meeting next week. Love, M.

9 January, (Wednesday) 6:00 pm

Hi Martin,

What do you think of this for #5?

5. GUEST TO INDEMNIFY OPERATOR

The Guest indemnifies and releases the Operator from any liability to any person except where the loss (or death) was caused or contributed to by the negligent acts or omissions of the Operator its servants, agents, contractors or sub-contractors.

It should keep them happy that something was included relating to risk. Anything to get them to agree!!!!

I will add it to the agreement unless you think I should leave the original #5 out completely.

They really do have a duty of care for anyone who is on their premises whether they are residents, guests or just visitors to the complex. Love, R.

PS. Do have a good night's sleep and wake up feeling like a million $. By the way - try putting a bit of Vodka into the soup and eat it hot! One never knows - it might work!

9 January, (Wednesday) 8:25 pm

I think that your statement would be better than removing #5 completely. M

9 January, (Wednesday)

Hi Roberta,

I am proposing to send this off to Michelle tonight/tomorrow ... any comments?

Happy New Year Michelle,

As you are probably aware the Christmas and New Year holidays prevented Roberta and I from getting Solicitor's advice as recommended in your covering letter.

However, we did meet with Michael Wright, Solicitor, on the Gold Coast today (9th Jan) and he has advised that some anomalies and omissions should be clarified and/or deleted/included in the document before we sign the licence. He is producing an amended licence that recognises the obligations on all parties in the agreement, not least the right of the 'resident' in the event of termination of the licence due to an irretrievable breakdown in the relationship. A factor not mentioned in paragraph 4.

Roberta and I would therefore like to meet with you to discuss and agree the way forward and, if in full agreement, sign the amended licence at that time.

We leave for a holiday in NZ on Saturday 19th January and would like to meet you on Friday the 18th sometime after 10.30 am if possible.

Could you please advise if this is possible, or suggest an alternative date. We return on Monday 4th February, but would obviously like to complete this signing activity before the moving date of 11th February 2008.

Regards

Martin Williams

(Love, Martin)

10 January, (Thursday) 8:18 am

Hi Martin,

Here's our version of the Guest Licence to present to Michelle. Let me know if you think anything should be changed. Love, R.

LONG TERM GUEST LICENCE *4

THIS DEED made the 18 day of January 2008

BETWEEN: WELLINGTON MANOR PTY LTD ACN 054 667 024 of Level 16, Waterfront Place, 1 Eagle Street, Brisbane in the state of Queensland ('The Operator')

AND: **ROBERTA CAVA** (de facto partner of Martin of Villa 3196, Wellington Manor, Wellington Point in the state of Queensland ('the Guest')

AND **MARTIN JOSEPH WILLIAMS** (de facto partner of Roberta) of Villa 3196, Wellington Manor, Wellington Point in the state of Queensland ('the Resident')

RECITALS:

A   The Resident is the lessee under registered lease no. 705068890 between the Resident and the Operator dated 30 August 2001 ('the Lease').

B.   Pursuant to the Lease, the Resident has the right to reside in Villa 3196 in 'Wellington Manor Retirement Village,' Wellington Point, Queensland ('the Village') as that villa is described in the Lease ('the Unit'). The Operator is the registered owner of the land in which the Unit is located and operates the village.

C.   The parties agree to allow the Guest to reside in the unit with the Resident on the terms contained in this licence.

1.   GRANT OF LICENCE

The operator grants to the Guest a licence to reside in the Unit jointly with the Resident on the terms contained in this licence.

2.   TERM

(a) The Licence commences on the date of this Licence.

(b) The Licence expires on the sooner of:

   (i) The death of the Guest; or

   (ii) The date that the Guest is required to vacate the Unit in accordance with Clause 4 of this Licence.

   (iii) The termination of the relationship of the Guest and the Resident.

3.   OCCUPATION OF UNIT

(a)   The Guest:

   (i)   Agrees to comply with and observe all the terms of the Lease (including any amendments to the same) during the term of the Lease and during any term that the Guest occupies the Unit under this Licence (including any time in occupation following the death of or vacation of the Unit by the Resident if applicable);

   (ii)   Agrees to vacate the Unit on the date that the Guest is required to vacate pursuant to Clause 4: and

   (iii)   Agrees to pay all payments and outgoings under the Lease including, but not limited to, any general service charges, maintenance reserve fund contributions or personal services charges during the term of the Licence (including any term in occupation of the Unit following the death of or vacation of the Unit by the Resident if applicable).

(b) The Resident acknowledges that:

   (i) Where following the death of or the vacation of the Unit by the Resident the Guest remains in occupation of the Unit, the Operator is under no obligation to locate a new resident for the Unit until the Guest vacates the Unit or where a date for the Guest to vacate the Unit pursuant to the terms of this Licence has been determined. Accordingly, the payment and calculation of the exit fee and exit entitlement (as those terms are defined in the Lease) and any other entitlements or payments under the lease payable on termination of the Lease may be postponed if the Guest elects to occupy the Unit (subject to the terms of this Licence) following the death or vacation of the Unit by the Resident; and

   (ii) the Guest may occupy the Unit following the death of the Resident (in accordance with Clause 4 of this Licence) which occupation may impact on the cost (i.e. by increasing the works and the costs of such works) relating to the reinstatement work (as that term is defined in the Lease).

4. **TERMINATION OF THE LICENCE**

(a) The Guest may terminate this Licence at any time during the term of this Licence by giving the Operator thirty (30) days prior written notice of their intention to terminate this Licence and vacate the Unit.

(b) The Operator may terminate this Licence:

   (i) If the Guest is in default of this Licence – by giving the Guest at least thirty (30) days written notice that this Licence is terminated and the Guest is required to vacate the Unit;

   (ii) If the Resident dies or vacates the Unit ('in this clause, collectively referred to as the 'Resident Leave Date'), and the Guest has prior to the Resident Leave Date occupied the Unit pursuant to this Licence for more than three (3) months, and the Guest is occupying the Unit at the Resident Leave Date – by the Operator giving the Guest at least three (3) months written notice that this Licence is terminated and the Guest is required to vacate the Unit;

(iii) If the Resident dies or vacates the Unit, ('in this clause, collectively referred to as the Resident Leave Date'), and the Guest has prior to the Resident Leave Date occupied the Unit pursuant to this Licence for less than six (6) months, and the Guest is occupying the Unit at the Resident Leave Date – by the Operator giving the Guest at least thirty (30) days written notice that this Licence is terminated and the Guest is required to vacate the Unit; or

(iv) The Resident, under the terms of the PID – if the relationship between the Guest and Resident is determined to cease, the Resident may give the Guest notice to vac ate within thirty (30 days.

5. **GUEST TO INDEMNIFY OPERATOR'**

The Guest indemnifies and releases the Operator from any liability to any person except where the loss (or death) was caused or contributed to by the negligent acts or omissions of the Operator, its servants, agents, contractors or sub-contractors.

6. **COVENANT**

This Licence is personal to the Guest and is not assignable to any other person or entity.

7. **GUEST'S RIGHT OF OCCUPATION**

The Guest has a personal right of the Unit on the terms contained in this Licence and has no legal interest in the land on which the Unit is situated on or the Unit or any right to exclusive possession of the Unit. The Guest acknowledges that she is not a 'resident' as that term is defined under the Retirement Villages Act 1999 (as amended from time to time), but has the full use of the facilities of Wellington Manor.

8. **OPTION TO PURCHASE**

The parties to this agreement, their heirs and assigns agree that the Guest may elect to purchase the Resident's interest in the lease upon his death subject to the usual terms and conditions of the Operator.

9. **COSTS AND STAMP DUTY**

The Guest shall bear her own costs of and incidental to the preparation, execution and stamping of this Licence and any ancillary documentation relating to the Licence and all stamp duty payable on this Licence.

IN WITNESS OF THE SAME this Deed has been duly executed.

EXECUTED BY WELLINGTON MANOR RETIREMENT VILLAGE PTY LTD ACN 054 667 024 as the Operator this ____ day of _____2007 in accordance with the Corporations Act:

_____

Director

_____

Director

SIGNED SEALED AND DELIVERED by **ROBERTA CAVA** as the Guest this ____ day of _____2007 in the presence of:

_____

A Justice of the Peace/Solicitor

SIGNED SEALED AND DELIVERED by **MARTIN JOSEPH WILLIAMS** as the Guest this ____ day of _____2007 in the presence of:

_____

10 January, 11:30 am

That looks fine to me. I am wondering whether to forward it to Michelle prior to our meeting as a courtesy??? A lot depends upon her reaction to the letter I have just sent!!

I could say this is a copy of the licence as amended by Michael Wright, Solicitor, for approval by Meridien.

What do you think? Love, M.

10 January

Hi Martin,

Well, the lawyer sure didn't waste much time - his bill came in the mail today, so it must have been mailed out just after we left!!

Total amount is $220 (included GST) Love, R.

10 January, (Thursday) 11:28 am

From: Michelle Smith *5
To: Martin Williams
Cc: Diane Brown
Subject: RE: Long Term Guest Licence

Dear Martin,

Happy New Year to you and Roberta!

I would be able to meet with you and Robert on Friday, 18 January. I am actually going to be at Wellington Manor that day (from 10.00 am) as I will be attending one of the informal gatherings of residents that Diane has organised.

At this stage, I do not know how long the meeting with residents will last as we have not held any as yet. What I propose, therefore, is to contact you again after the first couple of these meetings have been held to give you an idea as to how long the meetings are lasting and then schedule a time to meet with you and Roberta. Is this suitable to you?

I would also like for Diane to be present at the meeting with you and Roberta.

Kind regards,

Michelle Smith
General Manager, Queensland
AMP Capital Meridien Lifestyle

10 January, 12:22 pm

Dear Michelle,

That will be fine. It will allow Roberta time to travel up from the Gold Coast.

We will look forward to meeting you and Diane.

Thank you for your quick response

Kind regards, Martin

10 January, 12:25 pm

Dear Martin,[*6]
I have just realised that I mis-spelt Roberta's name in my email (I have actually referred to her as 'Robert').

I am very sorry.

Regards,
Michelle Smith

10 January, 12:34 pm

She certainly is polite isn't she! I think you should send her a copy of the guest licence so she has time to look at it before our planned meeting.

Cute that she refers to me as Robert (saw her retraction) - You (and the other residents) didn't know you were entering into a gay relationship did you??? Cheers, R.

10 January, 12:22 pm

Hi Martin,

When you get a reply to your report letter, send her another one enclosing the amended 'Guest Licence.' Let me know what you do. Cheers, R.

11 January, (Friday)

Dear Michelle,

A query on the interpretation of the Queensland Retirement Village Act 1999 has arisen that requires your advice please.

Having made a small amendment to paragraph 7, our solicitor now considers that under the term of the Act, by signing the licence (a contract) Roberta could be deemed to have qualified as a resident and that the statement in blue type below should either be removed or amended as shown in red. The relevant sections (9 & 10) of the Queensland Retirement Village Act 1999 are included for ease of reference with the areas under question highlighted in blue

Extract from Long Term Guest Licence

7. *GUEST'S RIGHT OF OCCUPATION*

The guest has a personal right of the Unit on the terms contained in this Licence and has no legal interest in the land on which the Unit is situated on or the Unit or any right to exclusive possession of the Unit excepted as stated in Clause 4. The Guest acknowledges that she is not a 'Resident' as that term is defined under the Retirement Villages Act 1999 (as amended from time to time), but has the full use of the facilities of Wellington Manor.

It is suggested that the following statement may be more appropriate:

The Guest acknowledges that she is a 'Resident' as that term is defined under the Retirement Village Act 1999 (as amended from time to time) and is entitled to the full use of the communal facilities of Wellington Manor Retirement Village and eligible to join the Wellington Manor Residents Association and/or the Association of Residents of Queensland Retirement Villages.

Extract from Queensland Retirement Village Act 1999

9. Who is a resident

A resident of a retirement village is a person who has a right to reside in the retirement village and a right to receive 1 or more services in relation to the retirement village under a residence contract.

10. What is a residence contract

(1) A residence contract is 1 or more written contracts, other than an excluded contract, about residence in a retirement village entered into between a person and the scheme operator.

(2) A residence contract includes any other contract (an ancillary contract) between the person and the scheme operator if the ancillary contract is dependent on, or arises out of, the making of the residence contract or another ancillary contract.

s 11 14 s 11

Retirement Villages Act 1999

(3) Without limiting the interests that a residence contract may be based on, a residence contract may be based on a freehold interest in an accommodation unit.

(4) To be a residence contract, a contract must-

(a) either-

(i) purport to give a person, or give rise to a person having, an exclusive right to reside in an accommodation unit in the retirement village; or

(ii) provide for, or give rise to, obligations on a person in relation to the person's or someone else's residence in the retirement village; and

(b) purport to give a person, or give rise to a person having, a right in common with other residents in the retirement village, to use and enjoy the retirement village's communal facilities; and

(c) contain or incorporate -

(i) a service agreement or an agreement to enter into a service agreement that includes a copy of the service agreement; and

(ii) if the contract includes an ancillary agreement that is not signed contemporaneously with the contract, an agreement to enter into the ancillary agreement

that includes a copy of the ancillary agreement; and

(d) restrict the way in which, or the persons to whom -

(i) the right to reside in the retirement village may be disposed of during the resident's lifetime; or

(ii) if the contract is based on a freehold interest in an accommodation unit—the resident's interest may be disposed of during the resident's lifetime.

Sorry to hit you with this Michelle, but it does seem as if there are grounds to review paragraph 7 of the Long Term Guest Licence. It's all a matter of interpretation of an Act that should be crystal clear. The right and freedom to be able to join either ARQRV or WMRA Inc is also an important factor for anyone living in a retirement village on a long term basis, as Roberta will be doing.

Would you please ask your lawyers to reconsider this paragraph and advise an amendment to suit all parties that I can forward to my solicitor for inclusion into the final draft.

Many thanks and regards

Martin Williams

11 January, 11:42 am

Hi Martin,

Well done ... .And she thinks seniors are daft unthinking people! This will give her rise to consider otherwise. You have put the facts in front of her - now she will have to act.

As they say here in Australia 'Good on ya mate!' Love. R

11 January, 10:32 am

Thank you for your email.*7

I am away on business on Friday, 11 January 2008 and the morning of Monday, 14 January 2008.

Please do not hesitate to contact me on (gave number).

Alternatively, I will respond to your email when I return to the office on the afternoon of Monday, 14 January 2008.

Regards,

Michelle Smith
General Manager, Queensland

11 January (Martin found out through a phone call from Michelle that I should have all the rights a resident has at the village once I sign the agreement).

12 January, (Saturday)

Hi Sweetie,

Herewith itinerary for our NZ trip as requested.

Have just returned from getting Lorna's birthday present and found a 3CD set of Australian Bush songs for Liz...including 'along the road to Gundagai' ... so that should be okay for her Oz day????

Feeling fully recovered now, so back to work!! Love, M.

Hi Martin,

I've made a stab at typing out our itinerary, but there's a lot of information missing. Can you fill in the blanks? I would like to include the phone numbers of the motels where we will be staying so I can leave the information with Shirley (in case she needs to get in touch with me about my rental unit). Thanks, R.

13 January, 6:41 am

Morning sweetheart,

I am off to cook the Sunday Brekkie so not available on messenger until after 10.30. Miss you, Love, M.

13 January, (Sunday) - I received an email from a man who had attended one of my seminars when I was living in Canada (mid

1990's). He enquired whether I could do a Customer Service and Dealing with Difficult People seminar for his company in Medicine Hat, Alberta. I sent a copy of that email to Martin.

Hi Martin,

It's good to know that people that attended my seminars about 10 - 15 years ago still remember me! Here's an email I got from a former participant: Cheers, R.

13 January, (Sunday) 1:00 pm

Looks like you will be in Canada for early spring? Well done. Will Helen have returned by then? Love, M.

14 January, (Monday) 7:30 am

Hi,

I told them that April wasn't a good time for me to go - that I preferred June. Will see what they say.

14 January, (Monday) 5:50 pm

Hi Martin,

Any word from Michelle about the Guest Licence? Miss you. R.

14 January, (Monday) 6:49 pm

Hi Sweetie,

I have just received this from Michelle.

We either need a very good lawyer or move out in the next three months!!

Miss you too, Love, M.

14 January, (Monday) 5:18 pm

From: Michelle Smith *8

To: Martin Williams
Cc: Diane Brown
Subject: RE: Long Term Guest Licence agreement

Dear Martin,

Thank you for your email.

We have sought legal advice on this particular matter and confirm as follows:-

The Long Term Guest Licence ('Licence') is not a residence contract for the purposes of the Retirement Villages Act ('Act'). To be a residence contract, Section 10(4) of the Act provides that the contract must purport to give an exclusive right to reside. The Licence does not purport to do this and, in fact, the Licence acknowledges that Ms Cava is simply residing jointly with you and Clause 7 confirms that the right is not an exclusive right to occupy the villa. We also note that the other requirements of Section 10(4) of the Act for a residence contract are not satisfied by the Licence - i.e. it does not contain a service agreement.

Furthermore, it is clear from the Act that it is not the intention of the Act that a relative who is granted the right to reside in an accommodation unit would be considered a resident for the purposes of the Act. By way of example, Section 52 of the Act provides the circumstances under which a resident may terminate their residence contract. It is clear that these provisions are not intended to extend to a resident's guest.

In particular, Section 70B of the Act, which was included in the 2006 amendments to the Act, makes a clear distinction between a resident's right to reside in an accommodation unit and a relative's right to reside in an accommodation unit. Section 70B(4) specifically states that the guest has all of the rights and liabilities of a resident under the Act only when they occupy the accommodation unit following termination of the residence contract pursuant to Section 70B(2) of the Act.

As previously advised, should Ms Cava wish to be considered a resident for the purposes of the Act, then the existing residence contract that you have entered into would need to be terminated and a new residence contract (in your name and Ms Cava's name) would need to be entered into. Of course, this will trigger payment of any exit fees under your current residence contract, the issue of a new Public Information Document to both parties and the payment of a new ingoing contribution.

Kind regards,

Michelle Smith
General Manager, Queensland
AMP Capital Meridien Lifestyle

[Readers: Please note the last paragraph where Ms Smith alleges that if I was to become a resident, a new residence contract would need to be entered into which would trigger payment of any exit fees under the current residence contract, the issue of a new Public Information Document (PID) to both parties and payment of a new ongoing contribution.]

This information is crucial for the incidents that happened within the next three weeks.

14 January, (Monday) 10:28 pm

Thank you for your response Michelle, I will forward it on to our solicitor.

I look forward to meeting you on Friday.

Kind regards, Martin

15 January, (Tuesday) 10:14 am

Hi Martin,

I have now prepared three copies of the Guest licence and two of the cohabitation agreement.

In the Guest licence, I've added a clause relating to our de facto relationship that could make a difference down the line. It reads as follows:

AND: ROBERTA CAVA (de facto partner of Martin) of Villa 3196, Wellington Manor, Wellington Point in the State of Queensland ('the Guest')

AND: MARTIN JOSEPH WILLIAMS (de facto partner of Roberta) of Villa 3196, Wellington Manor, Wellington Point in the State of Queensland ('the Resident')

What do you think? R.

15 January, 10:52 am

Hi Roberta,

I agree ... they can only throw it out!!!

I have been through the PID with a fine tooth comb and can find nothing to support our case, but it does mention the death of a partner and that the villa remains with the surviving member. Have you noticed that nowhere in the 'Act' does it mention re-marriage or moving in of a new partner. The whole act is slanted towards the 'owners' to the detriment of the elderly resident. Some law that is. No wonder ARQRV are constantly lobbying members of the State parliament for change!!

Are you going to bring the documents with you? Is there any merit in giving Michelle an advance electronic copy saying this is what we are prepared to sign, or do we wait until face to face?

I'm preparing for tonight's committee meeting at the moment.

Love, M.

15 January, (Tuesday) 2:47 pm

I'll bring copies of the documents with me - three copies of the 'Guest Licence' and two of the Cohabitation agreement. I would NOT send her an advance copy.

Is everything lined up with your neighbour (The Justice of the Peace) to witness the documents and is an appointment confirmed with Michelle? What time should I be at your place on Friday?

Hope your meeting tonight goes well. Love, R.

16 January, (Wednesday) 4:06 pm

Hi Sweetie,

I am in a hell of a rush at the moment but need to speak to you later this evening after the film night, so may be after 9.30!!

Still no time from Michelle because she is attending the morning tea and is not too sure how long they will go on for. Probably be around noon. I have arranged to sign docs at my neighbour (Justice of the Peace) at 10.30, so guess you need to leave home by 9 o'clock. Love, Martin

16 January, (Wednesday) 4:44 pm

Hi Martin,

I will be there early Friday morning. Still have lots to do - haven't started even thinking about what I will take on my trip. I have to drop off my books at my accountant on my way on Friday as well, so will try to get to her office about 9:00 am that day and leave from there (Oxenford).

Have you made arrangements yet for the phone line to be done? I thought we had done that, but wanted to make sure. I wasn't sure whether you were going to get someone or whether I agreed to have Telstra do it all? My mind is a sieve these days!

Talk to you tonight. Cheers, R.

17 January, (Thursday)

Hi Martin,

I can't believe it - I have all the proposals done (about 24 of them) and they're off to the three publishers - 2 in the USA and one in Austria. Have done my change of address for the post office, have my accounting ready to take tomorrow, copies of our agreements ready to go - car is packed with stuff. Whew have I been busy!

One thing I MUST do tomorrow is stop in at National Storage and sign up for the storage space! Don't let me forget! I also need to get a padlock for there before I move.

How are things going at your end? Love, R.

17 January, (Thursday) 5:56 pm

Dear Michelle,

Do you have a feel for what time we could meet tomorrow? Sometime around 12.30 in the Boardroom would suit us as we have to call in at a storage facility on the way back to the Gold Coast.

Kind regards

Martin

18 January – I drove to Martin's home. We took our documents to the Justice of the Peace for him to notarise then went to our meeting with Michelle Smith and Diane Brown. At this meeting we presented the signed and amended Long Term Guest Licence.

From the commencement of this meeting, Ms Smith systematically criticised and refused to accept virtually every amendment made by our solicitor. She further humiliated us by implying that we had wasted our money and that if I wished to live in the village it would be on her (Meridien's) terms with no give or take.

She said we had three choices:

1. We would sign the Long Term Guest Licence with very minor changes relating to what would happen if Martin died and be responsible for the $700 charge for the defective [and illegal] document.

2. If I wished to be considered a resident for the purposes of the Act, then the existing residence contract would need to be terminated and a new residence contract (in both our names) would need to be entered into. This would trigger payment of any exit fees under Martin's current residence contract. They would then issue a new Public Information Document (PID) to both parties and the payment of a new ingoing contribution.

3. I could stay in the villa for three weeks, leave for one day and again stay for three weeks.

Naturally I took exception to these ridiculous choices and was particularly turned off by Michelle's autocratic attitude and resented being treated in such a derogatory manner. I queried whether the Long Term Guest Licence was legal because nowhere in the Retirement Village Act was such a licence mentioned. It was at this point that Diane left the meeting room to find a copy of the Retirement Village Act.

I also commented to Michelle that I felt we should not have to pay the $700 they expected us to pay for a flawed Long Term Guest Licence and that we already had to pay our lawyer's fee to re-word that agreement to make it legal. A heated discussion ensued. I replied that there must be other suitable alternatives than the three options she had offered. She said there were only the three she had mentioned. I looked her in the eye and stated, 'Your attitude towards the residents 'stinks' and the three alternatives you've given me to move in are a load of 'crap.'

It was at this point that Michelle threatened to cancel the Long Term Guest Licence and refuse to allow me to join Martin in the village. I could not believe that she had threatened me with such a thing but I knew there was no use arguing with such an immovable, stubborn, un-empathetic woman. I collected all the copies of the licence and abruptly left the meeting room in tears.

After I left the room, I did not know that Martin had told Michelle that we would return to our solicitor and implement all of her objections, but that we would not be able to do this until we returned from our holidays on 2nd February – nine days before my planned move-in date.

[Ms Smith subsequently denies that he had agreed to re-instate her terms in the licence.]

I would not have agreed to those terms, but did not know that those comments had been made by Martin until much later.

We returned to Martin's villa and were both very upset at the events that had just taken place. We decided we would have to think how we were going to deal with the dilemma during our upcoming vacation. I thought we should phone Meridien directly to see if they could find an alternative solution.

I realised that I was supposed to sign the agreement with National Storage in Capalaba to store my surplus belongings that day. I explained the problems we had run into that day and they said I could hold off signing the agreement until closer to my moving date. Martin and I drove to Gold Coast in my car because we were leaving for New Zealand the next day from the Gold Coast Airport.

19 January, (Saturday) – Doug drove us to the Coolangatta Airport. Martin and I were both still upset by what had happened the day before. I couldn't believe that Meridien would condone the actions of their General Manager and allow her to stop me moving in with Martin. What grounds could she use? I fit all the requirements for someone to live in the village – I was the right age, I had an impeccable history, had never even been given a speeding ticket since moving to Australia ten years before. However, knowing what kind of person she appeared to be, we found ourselves being distracted from really enjoying our visit to New Zealand.

We arrived in Wellington Airport where we were met by Liz and David Smith who lived on the Kapiti Coast. The next few days they showed us many sites around the area.

23 January, (Wednesday) - Liz and David drove us to Wellington to catch the ferry to Picton. We picked up rental car and drove to Nelson – stayed at the Hotel Circa.

24 January, (Thursday) - Drove from Nelson to Franz Joseph (or Fox Glacier) – 489 km (7:45 hours). We stayed at Glow Worm Motel in Franz Joseph.

25 January (Friday) – Drove to Wanaca 287 km – (6 hours). We stayed at the Edgewater Resort Motel.

26 January, (Saturday) – Drove from Wanaka to Queenstown (via Arrowtown).

27 January, (Sunday) – Drove to Ernshaw.

28 January, (Monday) – Took a bus tour – Milford Sound – returned by air.

29 January, (Tuesday) – Left Queenstown – drove to Mount Cook 263 km (4 hours). Stayed at the Hermitage Aoraki Hotel.

30 January, (Wednesday) – Drove from Mount Cook to Christchurch (via Lake Terapo) 325 km (5 hours). We stayed Jan 30 – Feb 2 at Bellavista Hotel.

31 January, (Thursday) – We went to the Avon River Point Butanical Gardens.

We both agreed that even though we had been under a tremendous amount of pressure because of Michelle Smith's actions, we enjoyed our holiday and were as loving as ever towards each other. However we were both becoming more and more anxious to know how things would go when we returned to Wellington Manor.

CHAPTER 8
FEBRUARY, 2008

1 February, (Friday) – Went on an Akoroa Peninsula Tour.

2 February, (Saturday) - Returned car rental at 1:00 pm. Flew from Christchurch to Coolangatta – home at 4:30 pm. Doug picked us up at the airport. Martin stayed overnight at my home.

3 February, (Sunday) - Martin backed my car into my garage so he could load his suitcases, but banged my car against a post resulting in a dent in my left back bumper. This was a minor thing, so I was able to drive him home. It was raining heavily, so I had to drive carefully.

When we got to Martin's place he picked up his mail. In it was the following letter from Michelle Smith:

22 January, 2008 *9

Mr. Martin Williams
(address)

Dear Martin,

Proposed Long Term Guest Licence – Villa 3196 Wellington Manor Retirement Village

We refer to your correspondence of 17 December 2007 providing a copy of the proposed Long Term Guest Licence with respect to the proposed occupancy of Villa 3196 ('the Villa') by Ms Roberta Cava and to the meeting of Friday, 18 January 2008 at Wellington Manor Retirement Village ('the Village') between yourself, Ms Cava, Diane Brown and the writer.

We note that following your request for permission for Ms Cava to be granted certain occupancy rights in respect of the Villa, we delivered the terms of a proposed Long Term Guest Licence ('the Proposed Licence') to you under the aforementioned correspondence.

We further note that to date, the terms of the Proposed Licence have not been resolved and in particular, we understand from our recent meeting with Ms Cava that the terms upon which we are willing to grant the guest licence to Ms Cava are unacceptable to her and that she holds certain grievances about the Village and/or our operating of the Village.

As you may recall, clause 11.18 of your Lease provides for your right to have visitors stay in the Villa from time to time. Following your request, we had considered granting certain rights of occupancy to Ms Cava over and above your rights contained in clauses 11.18. However, as a result of Ms Cava's conduct at our recent meeting and the inability of the parties to agree on the terms of the Proposed Licence, we now confirm that we are not prepared to continue negotiations as to the terms of the Proposed Licence and further, we now formally withdraw our previous offer to grant a Long Term Guest Licence to Ms Cava.

We confirm that any future visits to the Village by Ms Cava will be governed by the terms of your lease and, in particular, please ensure that the notice requirements under clause 11.18 for intended overnight stays are adhered to. *[This meant that I had to report to her every time I stayed overnight in Martin's villa.]*

In closing we confirm that Meridien are committed to ensuring that all residents residing at the Village do so at their own volition and willingly enjoy the benefits of retirement community living.

Should you have any queries or require clarification on the contents of this correspondence, please do not hesitate to contact the writer.

Yours faithfully,

Wellington Manor Pty Ltd
Michelle Smith
General Manager, Queensland

Martin and I just stared at each other in disbelief. How could this happen? All our plans had been thrown out the window by this vindictive person who left me with the situation where in eight days I would have no place to live.

Martin decided to contact Michelle on Monday to see what could be done about the situation.

I was shaking as I drove back to the Gold Coast, absolutely furious at the actions of Meridien and vowed that I would reverse their decision. How dare they refuse me entry into their village – I was not a criminal, yet was being treated as one. It took me a long time to calm down enough to think of solutions to my situation. My major problem, of course was finding alternative accommodation. So I went on the internet and started looking for accommodation near Wellington Point where Martin lived.

3 February, (Sunday) 6:34 pm

Hi Martin,

I've been looking at available rentals in Birkdale, Capalaba and Wellington Point and there seems to be quite a few available. I'll wait till I learn what happens after you call 'the bitch' tomorrow,

Love, R.

3 February (evening)

Hi Martin,

Do you know the name of Michelle and Diane's boss? If so, I think you should contact him/her on Monday to sort this out. Do have a list of all the difficulties/expenses these two women have or will cause us by their punitive actions. Love, R.

3 February

Hi Martin,

Here is the scanned letter Meridien sent on December 17th.

Liz is back on the Gold Coast. I will be going over to her place for dinner tonight. She has offered her place for me to use for a while, so at least I will have a roof over my head if I choose to do that.

I'm reeling as you can imagine, and know you are too. Love, R.

(This letter is shown earlier – December 17th)

4 February, 9:47 am

To Michelle Smith
Cc: Diane Brown
Subject: Proposed Long Term Guest Licence

Dear Michelle,

At the conclusion of our meeting on Friday 18th January, when I and Roberta Cava presented a revised signed and notarised edition of the Licence, as advised by our Lawyer, it was our understanding that you (Meridien) did not accept all of the changes made to the original document. Following our discussions with yourself, we therefore agreed that we would contact our lawyer to reinstate all the content you wished to retain, despite the fact we did not fully agree with Meridien's viewpoint. Also, as we were leaving for a holiday the following day there may be some delay in finalising the licence. However, we managed to do this before leaving Australia and the resultant agreement (attached) has been prepared for your approval prior to us having it notarised and presented to you at the end of this week.

I was therefore extremely surprised and disappointed to receive your letter dated the 22nd January upon my return that, at this very late stage of the negotiations, you have withdrawn the option of a Long Term Guest Licence to Ms Cava, apparently because of a personal disagreement with her views. This despite my previously stating to you that Ms Cava was currently under pressure and having considerable problems with a large publishing company who have not paid the International royalties on her book sales for some four years, or more – hence her reaction to Meridien's demands for sums of money that, in our lawyer's opinion, had very little justification, given the fact that the licence would suit many retirement situations with very little adjustment and should therefore not attract as full charge on every occasion.

Following long discussions during our holiday, we are fully prepared to sign the attached agreement and would request that you revise your decision and allow us to spend the remainder of our lives in the harmony of Wellington Manor Retirement Village.

I have broken a hearing aid whilst on holiday, so must take it for repair this morning, but would like to discuss this matter further with you when I get back. My apologies for sending an email rather than a letter but, as Roberta's lease finished next Monday, time is of the essence to resolve this current impasse.

Yours faithfully,

Martin Williams

[Note: I was not aware that Martin had sent this information to her because I would not have accepted signing a document that contained in my (and my lawyer's eyes) illegal clauses.]

5 February, (Tuesday) 5:19 am

Hi Martin,

Sorry I missed your call last night. I crashed at about 8:00 and didn't even hear the phone ring (and the phone is on the table beside my bed!)

I have to get my accounting stuff early this morning from my accountant in Oxenford, so I too will be out for a while this morning. I've left feelers with rental people in Wellington Point, Birkdale and Capalaba, but most of their offices were closed so I had to leave messages. R.

5 February

Hi Roberta,

I have just received this interim reply from Michelle and I am seriously concerned that I will not be civil when she phones me later this morning!!! She seems to have a very selective memory.

I have to ask do you still wish to live in the village before I try to recover the situation. Give me a call as soon as you have calmed down so that I know how to proceed.

I am so sorry I ever put you into this situation. Love M

5 February, 7:03 am (From Michelle Smith)

Subject: RE: Proposed Long Term Guest Licence *[10]

Dear Martin,

My apologies for not being able to return your call yesterday afternoon. The meetings I was attending ran severely overtime.

I will contact you today to discuss your email.

In the interim however, I would like to make the following comments:-

1. We did not accept the changes your Lawyer made to the Long Term Guest Licence as it took away the rights that would have otherwise been afforded to Ms Cava under the Retirement Villages Act 1999, which were included in our original licence. Furthermore, the changes made to the Licence also deviated from what had been previously agreed to by yourself (e.g. the terms of the Licence, the payment of fees for the preparation of same etc).

2. Our decision to withdraw the offer of the Licence is not, as you have stated, because of a 'personal disagreement' with Ms Cava's

views. The withdrawal of the offer is because of Ms Cava's behaviour and comments at the meeting held on Friday, 18 January 2008 at which time Ms Cava made it abundantly clear that she does not fully support the lifestyle choice that is retirement community living; made incorrect comments about Meridien Retirement Living and its management of Wellington Manor Retirement Village; made incorrect comments about the provisions and applications of the Retirement Villages Act; made grossly exaggerated comments about fees charged by Hopgood Ganim Lawyers; and used profane language when referring to the Licence and the concept of retirement village community living.

3. The fees for preparing the Licence were in excess of $1,200.00. You are being charged $700.00 as previously advised. During our initial telephone conversation to discuss the terms of the Licence, I also advised you that the fee that you would be charged would not be the full amount as charged by Hopgood Ganim Lawyers. Your lawyers comments in relation to the Licence are not correct.

4. We were not advised by Ms Cava or yourself that you would meet with and instruct your lawyer to reinstate the original provisions of the Licence. In fact, the meeting came to an abrupt end when Ms Cava walked out of the meeting room without any further comment.

Kind regards,

Michelle Smith
General Manager, Queensland
AMP Capital Meridien Lifestyle

What rights was she talking about in #1? Why should we pay for a licence that had illegal clauses in it? Again Michelle lied (#4). And since when did the word 'crap' constitute a reason to ban someone from the village?

6 February (Wednesday) - My search for new place started Wednesday – and I had a feeling of panic because my movers were coming the next Monday. I was able to contact a few real estate agents and decided to drive down the next day to view a few homes.

7 February, (Thursday) 4 days before I have to move ...

I drove to Martin's. It was raining cats and dogs. We were supposed to meet a real estate agent at a unit in Capalaba (about 10 blocks away from where Martin lived) but she was not there and we could not get into the complex. We sat in the car for some time outside the complex. Finally the fellow who owned the unit (Patrick) opened the gate and we went into the visitor parking. Because of road flooding, the agent could not get through. The home was quite suitable and was available immediately. It was a two-story brick, three bedroom townhouse with a nice back yard and visitor parking next door. However, the back yard had about four inches of water in it. Patrick said he had never had that happen before. It was well below the level of the home and because I was so desperate, I signed a 6 month lease to move in on Monday February 11.

I contacted the moving people and told them of the new arrangements – contacted the storage people who were kind enough to cancel the agreement when they heard what Meridien had done to me. Then I drove home and continued packing.

9 February, (Saturday) 2:28 am

Subject: Meridien - Glen Brown

Hi Roberta,

Note the time of sending this ... 2.28am!! I have been working on this on and off all day (and night) to make it a non-confrontational letter to the CEO of Meridien.

Can you check that is a true record of the events and let me know if there are any inaccuracies?

I have sent a brief note to Michelle Smith asking for the exact 'profanity' you are supposed to have used!!! Love, M.

(See final letter he sent to Glen Brown dated February 10.)

9 February, 6:57 am

Hi Martin,

You poor thing - hope you were able to sleep after all that. It's a good letter - you certainly have a way with words. I have made a few minor changes, but think it could go as is. Are you going to email it? If you're going to mail it - I would date the letter Feb 8th and mail it right away so he gets it Monday. Cheers, R.

9 February, 8:32 am

Hi Roberta,

Thanks for the input. Unfortunately it has gone onto three pages and I don't appear to have a 'first page ONLY' command for the header!!

Re the date, I am not going to mail it until next week as I am seeing our ARQRV rep today and may wish to make some changes before sending by snail mail. I also want to give Michelle time to respond to my question re 'profanity', plus I would like to ask Diane about her recollection of it, before Michelle gets to her for back-up once Glen calls her in. It would be nice if I could state in the letter that 'I have spoken to Ms Diane Brown who has no recollection of any profanity being used during the meeting' That would cut the ground from underneath Michelle's feet!!!

Wonder what time I will get the call to collect the key today?

Love, M.

9 February, 8:45 am

Hi Martin

Re: header information. Just type in that information on the letter itself - don't put it as a header.

I think your ideas re: holding off sending the letter are very valid.

I will be making a phone call to Jasmine [Patrick's real estate agent for my rental property] this morning to confirm that she spoke with Patrick. She was supposed to get back to me Thursday or Friday after she spoke with him. He might be able to bring the keys directly to me seeing he is now living on the Gold Coast. I will keep you informed. Love, R.

9 February, 10:23 am

Hi Roberta,

Do you have Michael Wright's address or email? It might be prudent to send him a copy of the letter in case Meridien contact him ... anticipate all avenues?? Love, Martin

9 February, 3:33 pm

Whew - I'm so hot - have been working like a horse since early morning except for occasional breaks at the computer.

Here are Michael Wright's details: (I gave details.)

No email address given but you could phone his office and get it:

His bill was for $220.00

No word from Jasmine - I might call again. R.

(Martin did three drafts of his letter to Glen Brown - this is the final one.)

10 February 2008 *11

Mr Glen Brown
CEO AMP Capital Meridien Lifestyle
GPO Box 2484

Brisbane Qld 4001

Dear Sir,

I am writing to seek confirmation that it is a Meridien Lifestyle policy for your senior employees to impose restrictions on the rights of a resident living in a Meridien Lifestyle Retirement Village to bring a new partner into their home?

I am a 73-year retiree who has lived in Wellington Manor Retirement Village since August 2001. My wife died of cancer after a long debilitating illness in November 2004 after 44-years of marriage. Last year I met a single lady, Ms Roberta Cava, and after some 10 months decided to enter a de-facto relationship that was duly signed and witnessed. In late November, I informed the General Manager, Queensland, Ms Smith, that I wished to bring this lady into my home but that she did not wish to have her name added to my existing PID – thus ensuring that my estate received a full inheritance upon my death. Ms Smith helpfully advised that the best option was to bring Ms Cava into my home under the auspices of a Long Term Guest Licence to be prepared at a cost of $700 (a 3-page document) together with a car parking licence (8-pages) at a cost of $50 per month. Incidentally, the term, or use, of a Long Term Guest Licence is not recognised by ARQRV.

The alternative was (I quote)

'As previously advised, should Ms Cava wish to be considered a resident for the purposes of the Act, then the existing residence contract that you have entered into would need to be terminated and a new residence contract (in your name and Ms Cava's name) would need to be entered into. Of course, this will trigger payment of any exit fees under your current residence contract, the issue of a new

Public Information Document to both parties and the payment of a new ingoing contribution.'

When I stated to Ms Smith, in the hearing of the Village Manager, Ms Brown, that other residents in the village had re-married and that the original Manor Group had directed their lawyers to add the new partner as a village resident at low cost without adding (in some cases), their partner to the PID, I was told that this was against the law and should not have happened?

The Meridien Guest Licence was subsequently produced on 17th December with a covering letter strongly recommending that independent legal advice be sought before signing. Due to the Christmas summer holiday close down, it was the 7th January before we were able to implement this recommendation with Michael Wright, Solicitor. He advised that any agreement signed by the 'resident', 'guest' and 'owners' was in fact a contract, and not a licence, to allow relatives, carer's, etc., to move into a retirement village and be free to use the village facilities. He then recommended changes to protect both the 'resident' and 'guest' that were missing in the original document. He also stated that as the 'licence' was a template for many similar situations (relatives, carer's etc.) there should be no charge to the 'resident'. This is an important factor to what followed.

As a result of this implied agreement to allow Ms Cava to reside in my villa, Ms Cava terminated her rental at Varsity Lakes with effect 11th February 2008 and arranged Removalists for that date. This information was passed to Ms Smith for inclusion into the Car Parking Licence. At that time I also sold some of my furniture to make room for some of Ms Cava's furniture.

A meeting was then arranged with Ms Smith for 18th January – the day before Ms Cava and I were due to leave on a fortnight's holiday. At this meeting we presented a signed copy of the amend Long Term Guest Licence witnessed by a Justice of the Peace.

From the commencement of this meeting, Ms Smith systematically criticised and refused to accept virtually every amendment made by our solicitor. She further humiliated us by implying that we had wasted our money and that if we wished to live in the village it would be on her (Meridien's) terms with no give or take. Naturally Ms Cava took exception to this dictatorial attitude and resented being treated in such a derogatory manner. A heated discussion ensued, especially in relation to the charges for the 'licence' (note our Solicitor's comments) and the alternative of selling the villa with an exit fee of 30% and then re-purchasing at the new valuation. Ms

Cava stated that, in her view, Meridien were taking advantage of elderly persons who were captive to the terms of their PID agreement with retirement the village operator. Ms Smith took exception to this and stated that she was considering withdrawing the 'offer' of a Long Term Guest Licence. In an attempt to bring common sense to the situation, I said that we would return to our solicitor and implement all of Ms Smith's objections, but that we would not be able to do this until returning off holiday on 2nd February – nine days before the move in date. All copies of the original and revised copies of the licence were then collected and Ms Cava abruptly left the meeting in tears. Ms Smith subsequently denies that we had agreed to re-instate her terms in the licence.

Upon return from holiday I was devastated to receive a letter from Ms Smith stating that she was formally withdrawing the offer of a Long Term Guest Licence due to Ms Cava's attitude to retirement living. There was also a statement that Ms Cava had used a profanity. This is completely and utterly untrue. The strongest term used was 'that stinks!' in relation to Meridien obtaining money by forcing an owner to sell and then re-purchase their own villa, thereby getting two bites of the exit fee from the same person – a view taken by virtually everyone I have spoken to since receiving Ms Smith's letter. It may be legal but is it an ethical practice? I attempted to get Ms Smith to reconsider the contents of her letter and was told that even if I were to marry Ms Cava, she would not allow her to move into my home. What an unbelievably arrogant statement that was. Is it correct and supported by Meridien Lifestyles? This decision left Ms Cava with 6-days to find new accommodation!

I find it regrettable that an executive member of Meridien can be so insensitive to the needs of elderly residents in their care. I have previously admired the confidence and professional manner that Ms Smith showed when presenting the annual budget meeting, but must say I have no confidence in her ability to deal with elderly people, or accept criticism. Despite her denial, I believe that Ms Smith allowed her personal animosity towards Ms Cava to overrule her judgement. This has resulted in Ms Cava being put to considerable expense in finding new accommodation at very short notice and my having to replace furniture. More importantly, Ms Smith's decision to stop me from bringing a partner into my home is an infringement of my civil rights and I will be taking legal advice on this matter.

However, before doing so, I would like to know if you condone the actions taken by Ms Smith and whether you are prepared to resolve this situation? As a Lawyer, I am sure you will appreciate that there are two sides to every story and balance them accordingly. You will also be fully aware of the ways to exploit the loopholes in the Retirement Villages Act 1999, Queensland, as amended March 2007; therefore solicitors will interpret them to suit the requirements of their client.

I hope you will understand that I no longer wish to deal with Ms Smith on this personal matter, but I will not let this affect my dealings with her in my role as a member of the Residents Association Committee Executive.

Yours faithfully

Martin Williams

10 February, 11:21 am

Hi Martin,

Jasmine from LJ Hooker finally phoned - she has been away sick for two days. The owner left the keys in the house so she was going to pick them up and deliver them to your place. However, I discouraged her from doing so - because she says I have to sign the lease before I move in - which would mean I would have to go to her office and keep the movers waiting with the truck before I could move in. She will be emailing the lease to me and has agreed to meet me at the unit tomorrow morning- I'll give her the signed lease and she will give me the keys etc. So you won't have to pick them up.

The fellow also says he still has the bed in the unit. I told her I have two queen sized beds coming in and there is no room for it. He also has stuff in the shed (I don't remember seeing a shed do you?) I said the stuff in the shed can stay, but the bed has to go - at least out onto the patio as a last resort.

I will phone you soon after I arrive at the unit. Love, R

10 February, 11:46 am

Hi Roberta,

Hope everything is going ok with the packing. The small shed was in the corner of the courtyard where the water was rushing under the fence.

I would imagine that you would arrive at the unit some 15 minutes to half an hour before the removers arrive so I hope Jasmine is there at the appointed time.

Let me know if you need anything done. Love M

10 February 3.55 pm

Hi Martin,

I think I'm on top of things - although my back is killing me and I ache all over. Jasmine has not emailed me the lease agreement, so guess she will be delivering it tomorrow. So I have folded up my printers and scanner and have just left the basics hooked up till this evening. Have some of my computer stuff packed in the car already. Am going to treat myself and get take-away tonight. Love, R.

10 February 4:30 pm

Hi Martin,

I will be turning on my mobile phone early tomorrow morning if you want to get in touch with me. I still haven't heard from LJ Hooker so have no idea how and when I will get the keys for the unit. I'll need you to call them about 8:30 that morning to nudge them into doing something.

I certainly hope I won't arrive at the place and find I can't get into the unit because I will have no keys. I imagine that LJ Hooker must have their own keys at least, but won't have a zapper for the gate to enter the complex.

How are you today? Love R.

10 February, (Sunday). I was in the last stages of packing, but needed more empty boxes, so drove to a nearby shopping centre to get some. On the way back, I felt a terrible pain in my chest and had trouble breathing. I was only a couple of blocks from my home, so drove home. When I got inside I realised I was sweating profusely and felt a tightness in my chest. Heart attack – I thought and did as everyone had been told to do – phoned for an ambulance, unlocked the front door, had the gate opener in my hand as I sat in a padded chair facing the door where I could keep observation on the gate to the complex. I phoned Babette and asked her to phone Martin to let him know what had happened. I took my mobile phone with me and told her I would send her updates on how I was.

The ambulance drivers arrived, I opened the gate, they examined me and then took me into the ambulance. My next door neighbour came over when she saw the ambulance and asked whether there was anything she could do to help. I gave her a key to my place and asked her to lock up.

On the way to the hospital, the emergency services people realised that their heart monitor was not working so it was a very quick trip to the hospital where I was soon in a hospital bed hooked up to a heart monitor. A doctor came to read the printout and asked me some questions. Then he examined me and when he touched me on the chest-wall I winced and said that it was very sore. He touched other areas over my chest and front shoulders, and then announced that the electrocardiograph was normal except for an elevated pulse. I asked him what he thought caused the pain. He asked me what I had been doing before I had the pain and I explained that I was moving the next day and had been packing boxes all day.

He then said he thought I had pulled some muscles in my chest wall and to not lift any heavy boxes for a few days. Oh yeah! Try doing that when you're all alone and moving to a new location! However, I was very relieved that it wasn't my heart! That's all I would need!

I was discharged from the hospital and was able to phone Martin to give him an update. By this time it was 11:30 pm and I still had more packing to do – so I did it after taking a couple of anti-inflammatories the doctor had given me for the pain.

11 February, (Monday) - Mini Movers arrived to load the truck and I drove ahead while they had lunch. I got the keys and signed the lease and was ready when the movers came to unload. Martin joined me and helped me with some of the moving-in chores. I was elated when I learned that the phone had been hooked up. By this time, there was no water in the back yard as Patrick had promised. It did have a lovely back yard with both sunny and covered-in areas. Patrick had moved his bed into the back yard where it was under cover, but had not said when he would pick it up with the rest of his belongings in the shed. Over the next weeks I had to overcome several problems with the unit and it was not until the second week in March that Patrick finally removed his stored belongings.

12 February, (Tuesday) 10:40 pm

Hi Martin,

Here's something you might like to add to your letter to Michelle's boss:

It's unfortunate that Ms Smith has objected to the term 'crap,' because in North America this term means 'rubbish.' I used the term at our meeting on January 18th when Ms Smith would not budge on the three choices we had for my residency in Wellington Manor. That was when I used the term 'crap' meaning: 'What a load of rubbish!'

Ms Smith also explained that should we decide to marry, my partner would have to pay up to 42% of the value of the unit to Meridien and be forced to re-buy the unit 'at the going rate' - more rubbish.

Just a suggestion. R.

February 14

Hi Sweetie,

Herewith a copy of the letter I sent to ARQRV with copies of the attachments listed. I sent it by express post so Les (Les is the president of the Association of Residents of Queensland Retirement Villages) *will get it tomorrow and then pass it on to the solicitor, David Wise.*

I await the response with interest!!!

I am planning to look at furniture tomorrow and will then call in to collect the 'crap' in your courtyard ... .eat your heart out Michelle???

Thanks for my Valentine. Love M

14 February

Dear Les

In response to your request during our conversation earlier today, please find enclosed documents appertaining to my current problem with Meridien General Manager, Queensland, Michelle Smith.

The documents are numbered and listed as follows:

12 Nov '07 - Letter to Michelle Smith.

17 Dec '07 - Letter from Michelle Smith with original Long Term Guest Licence (LTGL)

18 Dec '07 – Email to Michelle Smith acknowledging the LTGL

10 Jan '08 – Email to Michelle Smith requesting a meeting

10 Jan '08 – Email in response agreeing to a meeting

11 Jan '08 – Email to Michelle Smith querying interpretation of Qld Ret Villages Act

14 Jan '08 – Email response from Michelle Smith

18 Jan '08 – Revised LTGL (with solicitors input) signed and witnessed by JP taken to meeting

22 Jan '08 (received 4 Feb) – Letter from Michelle Smith withdrawing offer of LTGL

Series of 'to and from' emails starting from page 4 for the correct sequence.

My first letter draft to the Meridien CEO to mediate – not sent

My second letter draft to Meridien CEO to mediate – again not sent

Copy of my Lease Agreement with Wellington Manor Pty Ltd signed 27/08/01

It will be appreciated that there were also phone calls on the above subject matter. In particular, during the sequence of emails listed in 10) Michelle refused to change her mind and in response to my asking what would her reaction be if I were to marry Roberta Cava, she stated that nothing would change as she would not allow Roberta Cava to be a resident. It was at this point I realised it was absolutely pointless trying to reason common sense with Michelle Smith!!

Would you please advise in due course what action I should take? I will hold back writing a tongue in cheek third draft to the CEO as the first stage of mediation until I have heard from you.

Yours sincerely

Martin Williams

15 February, (Friday)

Hi Martin,

Good luck with this. I was surprised at some of the wording - this letter sounds antagonistic - I thought you were going to be careful not to sound that way in any correspondence about Miss High and Mighty?

Could you please send me a copy of your second draft letter to Meridien CEO - I haven't seen that one?

I have to pop into National Storage this morning and will stop off at the bank to deposit my bond cheque for rental on my Gold Coast unit that arrived by mail yesterday. I will also ask the bank to discontinue our joint MasterCard. We can always apply for another one later. Cheers, R.

16 February, (Saturday)

Hi there,

I finally am hooked up to broadband! What a relief. Now I can hook up my web cam and actually speak to people - even those who live overseas (hopefully).

See you soon. Love, R.

16 February, (Saturday)

Hi again,

Just had a nice surprise - a beautiful bouquet of flowers was delivered with a card saying 'Thank you for looking after our house.' From Shirley and her two sons Russell and Mark who owned the unit I had just vacated on the Gold Coast.

She also informed me that I had left a whole drawer full of pots and pans in the kitchen. I guess the trip to the hospital must have affected me more than I realised. She has suggested that we meet at IKIA for lunch so she can bring them to me.

Also - I waited over an hour on 'ignore' on the phone, but finally spoke to someone at iinet about the broadband speed. The guy was a bit snippy when I told him I was only getting 32 kbps - said I must be mistaken. He checked my line and lo and behold there's a problem at the switching station (no apology for treating me like a nincompoop). He says the problem will be rectified later today. In the meantime everything will take forever. I'll concentrate on trying to find those clothes I am missing! Cheers, R.

16 February, (Saturday)

I met Shirley Redwood at IKIA for lunch to get pots and pans left at rental unit. I bought a small patio table and four chairs. Then drove to Martin's for dinner.

18 February, (Monday)

Hi Martin,

I had a lovely surprise this morning. A delivery man brought me a box from my financial analyst. I thought it was more information about the investments he was putting me in. It wasn't - it was a lovely gift basket with ladies toiletries - quite large and extensive. He is very thoughtful. I had kept him informed about the trials and tribulations we have been going through. I will call him soon to thank him.

Have run into another problem - one you helped me with before. When the movers took out the drawers in the filing cabinets - they lost many of the ball bearings so one drawer is impossible to use. I pulled it out and it nearly fell on my foot. I've taken everything out of the drawer and pulled it out but find there are no ball bearings on it - not sure what's happened to the rest of the drawers. Oh dear - what a lot of trouble this move has been!

Can I get more ball bearings at Bunnings? I hope the rest of the drawers don't have the same problem! Cheers, R.

18 February, (Monday) 9:14 am

Hi,

Just a reminder that Frank has booked the 3-day (2 night) trip to Stanthorpe for Mon 5th May to Wed 7th May at a cost of $365 per person. This price includes 3 days coach, all meals and accommodation and is paid to the Stanthorpe motel on the Wednesday morning. The itinerary includes visits to wineries, fruit farms and lavender farms in the granite belt area with a superb Italian dinner on one of the nights. Remember, Stanthorpe can have low temperatures at night, so rug-up!!

The coach picks us up early on the Monday morning and arrives back at around 5pm on the Wednesday, so it might be best to stay the Sunday night at my villa ... also the Wed night if you don't want to drive back after a long day.

Let me know asap if you have a problem. I must now book the cats into the cattery!! Martin

18 February, (Monday) 9:50 am

Subject: Re: Stanthorpe 5-7 May

Hi Martin,

Sign me up. From what you said, we pay at the end of the trip - correct?

I think this is the trip you mentioned to Babette and Doug. Did they say they wanted to go? They will be leaving on Feb 27th and will be away for 7 weeks, so doubt if they are interested in going. The cost might be a bit high for them as well. Do you remember what they said on Boxing Day? Cheers, R.

18 February, (Monday) 10:25 am

Hi Roberta,

Doug and Babette asked Frank to include them for Stanthorpe at the Boxing Day dinner, so he has!! I did give the date of 5 May to Babette on the evening they collected us from the airport and as nothing was said, I presume they are still intending to come along. As you will see, I included them on the email I sent to you, so I hope they don't disappoint Frank??

Yes, we pay at the motel before leaving on the return journey.

Re: your damaged office drawer - I doubt you will be able to buy loose ball-bearings of the correct size at Bunning's. I will have a look at the drawer next time I come over. Are you free this afternoon to go to Bunning's to look at light fittings?

I have to take a load of cardboard to the tip and could call and collect you afterwards? Love, M.

18 February, (Monday) 11:59 am

Yes – I have nothing special planned except unpacking more stuff. Let me know when you will come.

I do hope Babette lets you know soon whether they are coming or not. In case she doesn't call - here's here phone numbers: (gave number). Love, R.

19 February, (Tuesday) 8:45 am

Hi,

I have sent a priority email to iinet asking them about my broadband connection. On their web page it says I should be receiving about 8,000 kbps - and as you know I am receiving 32 kbps. Some difference! Everything is soooooo slow! Hopefully they will get back to me today with an explanation. Love, R.

20 February, (Wednesday) 10:14 am

Hi Martin,

Just got an enquiry from a school in Shepparton, Victoria asking me details about doing a seminar on Time Management for them on 7 April. Will let you know whether they decide to go with it.

Thanks for dinner last night - see you again tonight. Love, R.

20 February, (Wednesday) – Went to Martin's for fish and chip supper and movie.

22 February, (Friday) – The extra phone jacks were installed and my broadband upgraded.

23 February, Saturday – Martin installed the shade on my patio.

25 February, (Monday) 12:46 pm

Hi Roberta,

I have just had a call from Marie (and Kev) asking if we are free for dinner on Tue 1st April? It is a long way ahead and after Easter. I am free, how about you?

How's this for coincidence. Lorna was driving back from the airport yesterday (John at the wheel) as the old men were walking up for their Sunday paper yesterday!! He did a quick u-turn so I was able to hear that she had a very good meeting in Munich and managed to get into the city in the evenings. She also gave Emirates a good report. Apparently they are opening their own terminal at Dubai next month. Love, Martin

25 February

Hi Sweetie,

My note to ARQRV followed by Les Armstrong's response. Can only wait and see at present!! Love M

25 February, (Monday) 11:33 am

Good Morning Les,

I am just making contact to confirm that you received my letter dated 14th February, together with all of the documentation referring to Meridien Lifestyle refusing to allow my partner to live with me.

I am slightly concerned that I should not leave it too long before taking a first step in the complaints resolution procedure of writing to Michelle Smith's boss along the lines indicated by documents 11 and 12 in my submission to you. It could well be that David Wise will advise differently.

However, a short email to confirm that my documents are receiving attention is my main concern at present.

Kind regards,

Martin Williams

(Les's reply:)

Hello Martin

Your concerns have been passed to the ARQRV Solicitor seeking his advice on this matter. I expect his response very soon.

I will advise you when this has been received.

Regards, Les Armstrong

25 February, (Monday) 9:42 pm

Hi Martin,

As far as I know I will be here (Marie & Kev's). The only thing I have pending in April is that possible seminar in Victoria.

Glad you had a chance to talk to Lorna and that her meeting went well. Yes, Emirates is a good airline - very professional. Cheers, R.

25 February, (Monday)

Thanks for the Anniversary e-card. Was it a year ago we met at Harbourtown? Now that you have reminded me of the date I will have to remember it in future??

Make it up to you next weekend. Love, Martin

25 February, 11:10 pm

I am proposing to send the following to my UK family and friends. Do you think it is a good summation of the situation? Let me know what you think. Love M

26 February, (Tuesday) 6:17 am

Hi Martin,

I think it conveys your feelings and shows how peed off and frustrated you are at her. I refer to her as a thirty-something 'Miss High and Mighty.' I think I would add the information that this management firm has already had 27 tribunal cases and there are three others pending with ours being a fourth. Love, R.

26 February

Hi Roberta,

I have taken some of your points on board and restructured the letter.

Am off to play pool and will probably call you later if not too late.

Love M

26 February, (Tuesday)

Hi Sweetie,

Herewith copy of the letter I finally sent to family and friends in the UK.

You might like to forward it to your relatives and friends with your own comments, changes etc. Love, M.

(Martin's first draft of his letter to his UK friends had to be 'cleaned up' before he sent it, but he was very graphic in it about what he thought of Michelle Smith. He subsequently sent the following letter):

Dear All,

Sorry I have not been corresponding very much this year in thanking everyone for Xmas cards, calendars and letters etc., but I have been very busy resolving day to day problems and preparing documentation to fight a legal battle.

You will recall in my Christmas letter that I and Roberta were preparing for her to join me in my villa at Wellington Manor Retirement Village and that we were going through the process of making her a resident of the village as my de-facto partner. Because Roberta did not want to be added to my lease (thus ensuring that upon my death, Lorna would receive my full estate) the Operations Manager, a very self-opinionated, intransigent and self-centred young woman. who also calls herself General Manager Queensland (get the picture?) of the new village owners (AMP Meridien Lifestyles) suggested we sign a 'Long Term Guest Licence' (LTGL) at a cost of $700, whereby Roberta could live in my villa, but would not be a 'resident' under the Queensland Retirement Villages Act. She would have no legal protection against the owners in the event of an accident. The alternative was for me to sell my villa and pay the 'owners an exit fee of 30% of the property value' and then buy it back at the new value with Roberta's name added to the purchase lease, plus a new future exit fee of 36%!!! 'YES' believe it, or not, the Queensland Retirement Villages Act regulations are so inept in favour of 'village owners' that this can be done!! Our old village owners never descended to that level of greed and allowed widowed/widower residents to take a new partner at very little legal cost.

Just before the Xmas holiday, which lasts until the second week of Jan out here, we received a LTGL with a recommendation that we seek the advice of a solicitor. This we did and he tore it apart because there was a complete lack of protection for either Roberta, or myself ... everything being in favour of the 'village owners', so he recommended several changes before we signed it. As we were due to take a holiday in New Zealand to visit friends on the 19 Jan, I arranged a meeting with the General Manager for the day before we left on holiday. We took along our revised LTGL, signed and notarised by a JP, in the expectation that it would be accepted. Imagine my chagrin when Ms Smith and her assistant (Village Manager of similar unhelpful disposition) rejected every change and proceeded to try and humiliate and dominate us with the 'favour' they were offering. The conversation became heated and Roberta told them a few home truths about the sheer greed of Meridien Lifestyles and used the word 'crap' to describe the morals of the Meridien ethics towards retired seniors.

We left the meeting in a high state of dudgeon and agreed that upon our return from holiday we would have the LTGL returned to roughly its original state and sign it before moving in on the 11th Feb. - 7 days after the holiday. At this point, Roberta had cancelled her lease on the Gold Coast, arranged a removal firm and booked long term storage of some of her furniture and effects. On my part, I had sold some of my furniture to make space for Roberta's furniture and arranged for power points and telephone point in my dining room that I was converting into an office for Roberta's company HQ.

On Monday 4th Feb, I returned home to find a letter from the General Manager stating that she was 'officially' withdrawing the LTGL and that Roberta was not allowed to live in the village because of her profanity (the word 'crap') and her attitude towards Meridien Lifestyles!! When I contacted the Ms High and Mighty Smith by letter and phone, she flatly refused to change her mind and stated that even if I was to marry Roberta, she would not be allowed to move into my villa. She also denied that we had agreed to put the LTGL back to its original one-sided format before the move in date. At this point I realised it was absolutely pointless trying to reason with someone as vindictive as the 'cow'... an expression that Marguerite would have used!!?

As a result of this vindictive decision, we were then left with five days to find new rental accommodation for Roberta. Luckily we managed to find a small gated community about five miles away and Roberta moved in on the 11th Feb and is now relatively well settled for the next six months. In the meantime, I have taken advice and sent a full resume of all the correspondence and sequence of actions taken to a lawyer who specialises in protecting residents of retirement villages who have bad dealings with 'village owners'. I have subsequently had to buy new furniture giving me a loss of over $1000. Not a happy situation given that my frozen UK pensions are now transferred at their lowest exchange rate against the strong Aussie dollar for some fifteen years!! The plus side is that Roberta and I are living much closer to each other and can meet-up in 10 minutes plus it is easy for her to attend village entertainment functions.

It is worth noting that AMP Meridien Lifestyles only entered the Retirement Village industry in the last two years, or so, with a very aggressive policy of purchasing of villages throughout Australia and have now become one of the big players owning at least 26 villages, five or more, of which are in Queensland. They obviously saw it as a very lucrative business with the exit fee on the re-sale of villas when the owners die off. They even raised the exit fee from 30% to 36% for all new incoming residents to ensure their profits increased for the benefit of shareholders.

They have also curtailed some of the benefits the residents used to enjoy from the previous owners, especially in this village. Xmas dinners, inter-village BBQ's etc. Given that attitude, it is not surprising that some of its employees have prison warder mentality towards their dealings in the treatment of elderly residents and this is reflected in the increased number of complaints against Meridien being received by the ARQRV (Association of Resident of Retirement Villages Queensland). This is the only association that can provide some measure of protection for residents of retirement villages. They arrange legal advice for complaints proceedings, often leading to a Tribunal hearing against the respective 'village owners'. It is this organisation that is now considering my case along with, as I understand it, two other similar cases also against Meridien, plus some 24 other complaints which may reach a tribunal if not settled out of court.

We had a good holiday in NZ and I may tell you about it sometime when things get settled at this end.

Sorry for the self-centred news but felt you should be aware of what is going on in some detail. Naturally, I am not a happy chappie at the moment.

Love and best wishes, Martin

28 February, (Thursday)

Hi Roberta,

Angela has booked a table for 12 at the Mates Theatre on Sat 19th April for the play 'A Mid Life Crisis' and would like to know if we can attend. Do you wish to go providing you are not in Canada?

I have confirmed we are okay for Marie and Kev's dinner on Tues 1st April. Is that one a lunch or dinner? *Martin*

29 February, (Friday) 9:00 am

(Email from one of Martin's neighbours)

To: Martin Williams

Subject: Re: Retirement Villages Act

Hi Martin

Thanks for that. Ken, Don and I already have a hard copy of the act but it will be good to have more.

On a lighter note - Prince Harry was interviewed in Afghanistan this morning. He used the word 'crap' several times along with other words. If it is good enough for the third in line to the throne it should be good enough for Ms. Smith!

Bye

Ruth and Arthur Kelleher

CHAPTER 9
MARCH, 2008

7 March, (Friday)

Hi Martin,

My financial advisor phoned me this morning to answer my question about my AMP investments. He says there are other investments that are paying just as well. So I've given him instructions to sell all my AMP investments. In the meantime, I have written the following letter (but haven't sent it yet) to the Head office of AMP.

Let me know if you think I should add anything else to the letter.

Cheers, R.

7 March, 2008 [12*]

AMP

33 Alfred SSW 2000'
Attn: Craig Dunn, CEO
Re: Managed Investments

I have managed investments under Navigator Personal Retirement Plan as follows:

(I gave account information). Value $87,916.58

I will be pulling out of that investment because of the unforgivable way AMP Capital Meridien Lifestyle Retirement Village Operators have treated me. I was to move into Wellington Manor Retirement Village to live with my partner and Ms. Michelle Smith, General Manager, Queensland of the Meridien Management group decided that I was not suitable to live there because of a personal disagreement. I was informed of that decision on February 4th, exactly one week before I was to move in with my partner. I had a moving truck coming on February 11th and found myself with no home to go to.

Therefore I will be pulling out my shares and I'm sure you can understand that I have every reason not to trust either AMP or Meridien by the way they treat seniors.

Sincerely,

Roberta Cava

7 March, (Friday) 9:54 am

Hi Roberta,

A very good letter my dear. I have made a couple of comments for you to consider as they should be aware of the personal animosity. Also, are you sending it to the CEO of AMP?

Busy at the moment so will speak to you later. Love, Martin

7 March, (Friday)

Hi Martin,

I have addressed my letter to Craig Dunn, the new CEO of AMP. I'm wondering if you should ask the other residents whether they too have AMP shares in their portfolios. I don't care if you show my letter to them - if everyone pulls out of their shares with AMP and send them a letter explaining why - it might have a small impact on their actions.

Just a suggestion. R.

7 March, (Friday)

Good morning Les,

I was rather disappointed after our conversation the other day in that David Wise did not think we had grounds for a Tribunal against Meridien. Did he get a copy of all of the documentation I sent, especially the actual statements made by Michelle Smith? Roberta is extremely upset that there is direct discrimination against her. Given the fact that many of Wellington Manor Residents were expecting Roberta to move in with me, Meridien's late refusal to allow her to move in could be construed by many who do not know the full circumstances that there must be a reason, such as a police record, or similar!!

The fact that Meridien have prevented me from bringing a new partner into my home is a direct breach of my civil liberties. Surely there must be grounds to challenge their decision?

Turning to the other element of our discussions on Monday regarding the formation of a non-association Residents Committee. This is now going ahead and I have attached a confidential copy of a report I intend to include in the minutes of an Association Committee meeting next Tuesday. I would welcome your comments if you spot any inaccuracies. I would stress again that this is currently confidential advance information.

Finally, Eric Stadhams, our ARQRV representative, has sent our association secretary a letter asking for us to contact you to arrange for you to come and talk to the residents of Wellington Manor. We will probably pass this on to the new residents committee when elected. However, if this is an ARQRV presentation there is nothing to stop Eric from selecting a date, booking the hall and circulating a flyer (funded by the association) to notify residents. We (the two committees) would then ask for a separate meeting with you to discuss our current situation. We would wish to restrict this to 2 members of each committee so that the questions would be more focused. Do you have an opinion on this?

Kind regards

Martin Williams
Acting President
Wellington Manor Residents Association Inc.

8 March, (Saturday) 4:37 pm

Good Morning Les,

Martin and I would like to meet with you (and Phil if he's free) to discuss how things are likely to proceed from this point onward with our dispute with Meridien. Both of us are free to visit you next Thursday and wonder if that would be suitable for you.

A friend of mine wants to set up a meeting with an award winning American journalist who now works for the Courier Mail to discuss Meridien's actions towards Martin and me. The interview would likely be in April some time. We are wondering if you would also like to be interviewed at the same time. However, we don't want to jeopardise anything that might hurt our case against Meridien by being premature in discussing this issue with the media.

I would also like to meet you to see how we could work together in writing a book entitled 'Dealing with Retirement Village Bullies.'

I look forward to hearing from you about the proposed meeting for Thursday at Buddina.

Best regards,

Roberta Cava

9 March, (Saturday) 10:14 am

Hello Roberta

Each of your proposals sound great. I am certain that Phil and I will be able to identify the difficult operators, because the vast majority of them fit into that category, moreover the only way that we have found to deal with them is to initiate the Dispute Resolution process. If our case is strong (and it usually is) in almost every instance when the SO is breached the Act they capitulate before the final Hearing. Unfortunately, neither Phil nor I will be available on Thursday next; I will be attending a National Seminar of Retirement Village Residents in Melbourne and Phil will be undergoing a final check for an eye problem. On my return I shall contact you to arrange a mutually convenient date, sooner rather than later.

Regards, Les

9 March, (Saturday)

Hi Martin,

I've just sent the following message to Jasmin - wonder if it will receive a reply? R.

12 March, (Wednesday) 8:26 am

Hi Martin,

How did your meeting go yesterday?

Will you be able to come for dinner tonight? Love, R.

12 March, (Wednesday) 9:43 am

Hi Roberta,

The meeting went very well (just an hour) and Ken and I were able to finalise the minutes last night and will be distributing them later this morning.

I would love to come to dinner tonight and will get to you sometime after 5.30 if that's okay with you?

I had to take my XP computer in for repair. It was really playing up and finally refused to boot-up due to a power problem (flashing green light and no picture). I hope to get it back later today.

Any response from Hookers? Love, M.

12 March, (Wednesday) 12:20 pm

Hi Martin,

5:30 would be fine. Sorry about your computer - they always seem to cause trouble don't they? Maybe it wasn't your keyboard that was at fault after all.

See you later. Love, R.

13 March, (Thursday)

Good morning sweetheart,

Thanks for dinner and your company last night, it was what I needed.

Brian has sent me 2 tickets for a St Patrick's Day Master Chef meal on Fri 28th March. Are you Okay for that? Love, M.

14 March, (Friday) – I joined the Redlands Probus Women's group

14 March, (Friday) 1:38

Hi Martin,

No word from L.J. Hooker, so I have sent them a fax to encourage Patrick to remove his belongings.

Did you want me to come to Happy Hour tonight? Love, R.

15 March, (Saturday) 4:40 pm

Sorry I am so late coming back to you ... I have been quite busy and have not looked at my mail. Am off to the Leisure centre ... have a meeting before happy hour. Ok if you come but probably too late!!!! WE should be outside around the back if you do come. Love, M.

15 March, (Saturday) – I paid $144 to have filthy windows power washed – will not be reimbursed – another expense to add to those caused by Meridien's cruelty.

19 March, (Wednesday) 3:53 pm

Hi Martin,

I talked to Doreen and Norman in Tamborine Mountain - we are invited for lunch on Sunday noon. Cheers, Roberta

19 March, (Wednesday)

Martin and I attended the film night at the village that showed my friend Elaine Hollingsworth in the film Magnificent Obsession (she played the part of the 'tart' at the beginning of the film).

19 March, (Wednesday)

Good morning Les, (with his answers)

Thank you for sending a copy of the constitution for a Residents Committee.

Wellington Manor held an inaugural meeting of residents on Monday and appointed a Procedures Committee to ask for, and process, nominations for the proposed new residents committee. I have passed your constitution template to the Secretary of the Procedures Committee and he will pass it to the chair of the new committee after the election process has been completed.

Re the ongoing situation regarding Meridien Lifestyles (Michelle Smith) refusing to allow Roberta Cava to move into my villa as my partner. Roberta has researched two other Acts that seem very applicable to our case and could well, in our opinion, overrule the Retirement Villages Act.

Many residents in this village who were aware that Roberta was going to move into my home are probably unaware of the reason she was refused and could assume that she has something in her background, such as a police record!! It is also an invasion of my civil liberties when Michelle Smith prevents me from bringing a de-facto partner into my home on a full time basis. Could you please confirm that the ARQRV solicitor is considering this approach?

Also, I am still unsure whether I need to send a letter to the CEO of AMP Capital Meridien Lifestyles to ask him to mediate before taking any legal action. Could you please advise.

I hope the Melbourne Seminar was useful.

Regards, Martin

Here is the relevant information from the Human Rights Act 2004 and Anti-Discrimination Act 1991

Human Rights Act 2004 [*13]

Part 3 Civil and Political rights

8. Recognition and equality before the law

1) Everyone has the right to recognition as a person before the law.

2) Everyone has the right to enjoy his or her human rights without distinction or discrimination of any kind.

3) Everyone is equal before the law and is entitled to the equal protection of the law without discrimination. In particular, everyone has the right to equal and effective protection against discrimination on <u>any</u> ground.

12. Privacy and reputation

Everyone has the right –

(a) not to have his or her privacy, family, home or correspondence interfered with unlawfully or arbitrarily; and

(b) <u>not to have his or her reputation unlawfully attacked</u>.

16. <u>Freedom of expression</u>

(1) <u>Everyone has the right to hold opinions without interference.</u>

(2) <u>Everyone has the right to freedom of expression.</u> This includes the freedom to seek, receive and impart information and ideas of all kinds, regardless of borders, whether orally, in writing or in print, by way of art, or in any other way chosen by him or her.

Queensland Anti-Discrimination Act 1991 [*14]

PART 2 Prohibited grounds of discrimination

7 Discrimination on the basis of certain attributes prohibited

The Act prohibits discrimination on the basis of the following attributes –

a) Sex;
b) <u>Relationship status;</u>
c) Pregnancy;
d) Parental status;
e) Breastfeeding;
f) Age;
g) Race;
h) Impairment;

i) Religious belief or religious activity;
j) Political belief or activity;
k) Trade union activity;
l) Lawful sexual activity;
m) Gender identity;
n) Sexuality;
o) Family responsibilities;
p) Association with, or relation to, a person identified on the basis of any of the above attributes.

PART 3   Prohibited types of discrimination

9. Discrimination of certain types prohibited

The Act prohibits the following types of discrimination –

a) Direct discrimination;

b) <u>Indirect indiscrimination</u>.

10. Meaning of direct discrimination

1) Direct discrimination on the basis of attribute happens if a person treats, or proposes to treat, a person with an attribute less favourably than another person without the attribute is or would be treated in circumstances that are the same or not materially different.

2) It is not necessary that the person who discriminates considers the treatment is less favourable.

3) <u>The person's motive for discriminating is irrelevant</u>.

4) If there are 2 or more reasons why a person treats, or proposes to treat, another person with an attribute less favourably, the person treats the other person less favourably on the basis of the attribute if the attribute is a substantial reason for the treatment.

5) In determining whether a person treats, or proposes to treat a person with an impairment less favourably than another person is or would be treated in circumstances that are the same or not materially different, the fact that the person with the impairment may require special services or facilities is irrelevant.

11. Meaning of Indirect Discrimination

1) Indirect discrimination on the basis of an attribute happens if a person imposes, or proposes to impose, a term –

a) With which a person with an attribute does not or is not able to comply; and

b) With which a higher proportion of people without the attribute comply or are able to comply; and

c) That is not reasonable

2) Whether a term is reasonable depends on all the relevant circumstances of the case, including, for example –

a) The consequences of failure to comply with the term; and

b) The cost of alternative terms; and

c) The financial circumstances of the person who imposes, or proposes to impose, the term.

3) It is not necessary that the person imposing, or proposing to impose, the term is aware of the indirect discrimination.

4) In this section –

Term includes condition, requirement or practice, whether or not written.

PART 4   Areas of activity in which discrimination is prohibited

Subdivision 1 – Prohibitions in accommodation area

81 Explanatory provision (prohibitions)

A person must not discriminate in the accommodation area if a prohibition in sections 82 to 85 applies.

82 Discrimination in pre-accommodation area

A person must not discriminate against another person

a) <u>By failing to accept an application for accommodation;</u> or

b) By failing to renew or extend the supply of accommodation; or

c) <u>In the way in which an application is processed;</u> or

d) <u>In the terms on which the accommodation is offered, renewed or extended.</u>

83. Discrimination in accommodation area

A person must not discriminate against another person

a) In any variation of the terms on which accommodation is supplied; or

b) <u>In denying or limiting access to any benefit associated with the accommodation;</u> or

c) In evicting the other person from the accommodation; or

d) <u>By treating the other person unfavourably in any way in connection with the accommodation</u>

84. Discrimination by refusing to allow reasonable alterations

85. Discrimination by refusing to allow guide dog

129. Victimisation

A person must not victimise another person.

Maximum penalty –

a) In the case of an individual – 45 penalty units or imprisonment for 3 months;

b) In the case of a corporation – 170 units.

130. Meaning of Victimisation

1) Victimisation happens if a person (the respondent) does an act, or threatens to do an act, to the detriment of another person (the complainant) –

a) Because the complainant, or a person associated with, or related to, the complainant –

i. refused to do an act that would amount to a contravention of the Act; or

ii. in good faith, alleged, or intends to allege that a person committed an act that would amount to a contravention of the Act; or

iii. is, has been, or intends to be, involved in a proceeding under the Act against any person; or

b) Because the respondent believes that the complainant, or a person associate with, or related to, the complainant is doing, has done, or intends to do one of the things mentioned in paragraph (a)(i), (ii) or (iii).

2) In this section, a reference to involvement in a proceeding under the Act includes –

a) Making a complaint under the Act and continuing with the complaint, whether by investigation, conciliation, hearing or otherwise; and

b) Involvement in a prosecution for an offence against the Act; and

c) Supplying information and producing documents to a person who is performing a function under the Act; and

d) Appearing as a witness in a proceeding under the Act.

[I felt the above information would be helpful if I took Meridien to court for slander and defamation of character.]

19 March, (Wednesday)

Hi Martin,

Sure hope Les gets things moving soon - it's been a month since you first notified him isn't it?

Here's a letter I received today from Glen Brown in reply to my letter to AMP. Absolutely no help at all! What a bunch!

Cheers. R.

19 March, 2008 *[15]

Ms Roberta Cava
(street address)
Capalaba Qld. 4157

Dear Ms Cava,

Proposed Long Term Guest Licence – Villa 3196 Wellington Manor Retirement Village

I refer to your correspondence of 7 March 2008 to Mr Craig Dunn of AMP Capital Investors in relation to our decision to withdraw the offer of a Long Term Guest Licence with respect to Villa 3196 Wellington Manor Retirement Village.

Mr. Dunn has asked me to respond on his behalf.

Upon receipt of your correspondence, AMP Capital Investors requested a full investigation of the matter, including our decision to withdraw the previous offer made following a meeting on Friday, 18

January 2008 at Wellington Manor Retirement Village between yourself, Mr Martin Williams, Ms Diane Brown and Ms Michelle Smith.

I have fully reviewed the results of these investigations and confirm that all ACML staff involved have acted appropriately and that our decision to withdraw the previous offer stands.

Yours faithfully,

Glen Brown CEO

At no time did they investigate our side of the story. What a one-sided investigation that was!

It was about this time that I obtained information on how a person could dispute a ruling by the village operators. Here is some of that information:

Chapter 5 – Dispute Resolution Information [*16]

General

1.5.1   Dispute resolution for a retirement village dispute between a resident and a scheme operator is available under the provisions of the Act. This dispute resolution process does not apply to disputes between residents or to disputes relating to the operation of a body corporate.

1.5.2   An attempt to resolve a dispute must first be made by the parties as an internal process. Parties are encouraged to use this process early to open up communication. If the dispute cannot be resolved, the parties can seek to have the dispute mediated and, if mediation is not successful, a dispute can be referred to the Retirement Villages Tribunal.

[We had tried to negotiate with Michelle Smith, but she went so far as to say that even if we married, I was not welcome in the village. So our next step was to contact Les Armstrong, the President of ARQRV (Association of Residents of Queensland Retirement Villages) to start proceedings to go to arbitration.]

Preliminary Negotiation

1.5.3   This first step is an internal negotiation process as outlined in Part 5 Chapter 4. The parties must first try to resolve the dispute by either party giving the other notice stating the matters in dispute and nominating a day for a meeting. The day nominated must be after a period of 14 days from giving notice.

1.5.4 The party receiving the notice must give a written response within 7 days of receiving the notice.

1.5.5 The parties must then meet to attempt to resolve the dispute.

1.5.6 The Internal Dispute Resolution at the village is described in Part 5 Chapter 4.

[We were not able to arrange this with the Owners, because the dispute involved me moving in with Martin within seven days. Martin did try to negotiate with her on the phone for two days, but she would not budge.]

Mediation

1.5.7 Disputes can be resolved by mediation, which is also an informal process. An application must be made to the chief executive of the department administering the Act for a mediator to be appointed to assist the parties to resolve the dispute. A mediator is then appointed to assist the parties to resolve the dispute. Details about the chief executive are set out below.

1.5.8 The types of disputes that can be mediated under the Act are all disputes other than:

- Disputes that are subject to arbitration;
- Disputes that are subject to an arbitration award;
- Disputes that are either before3 the court or that have been decided by a court;
- Disputes between residents; or
- Disputes relating to the operation of a body corporate.

1.5.9 Mediation can only be used if the parties have tried to resolve the dispute using the internal negotiation process first.

1.5.10 A lawyer or agent may represent each party at a mediation conference unless the mediator thinks a lawyer or agent should not represent a party. The mediation conference is held in private and no official record is kept.

1.5.11 A party to the dispute cannot be compelled to attend mediation.

1.5.12 Other persons may take part in the mediation if the mediator thinks the person has sufficient interest in the dispute.

1.5.13 If an agreement is reached on the dispute, the parties must sign a mediation agreement.

Tribunal Hearings

1.5.14 If:

- The parties cannot reach agreement; or
- One party does not attend mediation; or
- If the dispute is not settled within four months; or
- If a party claims another party to a mediation agreement has not complied with the agreement within the specified time or within 2 months of the agreement if no time is specified.

A party can apply to the Chief Executive to refer the dispute to the Retirement Villages Tribunal.

[Both Martin and I sent letters to Glen Brown, the CEO of AMP Capital Meridien. We were advised that they investigated the situation, but at no time did they discuss the matter with us to learn our side of the situation. There was no mediation – no discussion – and no signed mediation agreement. So we did try mediation, but it was a farce. We counted on Les Armstrong and the Resident Association lawyer David Wise to set up an arbitration hearing.]

What a frustrating dilemma this has been! I was becoming more and more angry at the way we were being treated by Meridien.

20 March, (Thursday) – I attended the Happy Hour at Martin's village in the Leisure Centre.

21 March, (Friday) - I had dinner at Martin's (Good Friday)

22 March, (Saturday) – I had dinner at the Leisure Centre with four couples, Martin and I, Frank and Amelia, John (can't remember her name) Barry and Wanita. It was a lovely evening.

22 March, (Saturday)

Hi Martin,

I am preparing information to approach the Courier Mail. One document I don't have is a copy of the letter you received cancelling the guest licence dated January 22nd. Could you please send me a copy of that letter? Thanks, R.

23 March, (Easter Sunday) – Martin and I drove to Mount Tamborine and had lunch with my friends Doreen and Norman.

24 March, (Monday)

I submitted a letter to Probus Club News for publication about our situation.

Here's the letter that includes Martin's additional information.

Attn: Jane Campbell

You might like to publish this in the 'Letters' section of the Probus Magazine.

The letter submitted by Peter Boam in your last edition was so true. He stated that retirement villages are populated by far more women than men and the trauma they went through losing a partner or pet. Also, many of the retirement villages where they live have contracted exit fees of between 30% and 36%, additional charges for refurbishment and resale can push this to around 50% of the value of the property.

What many of those single women (and men) might not know is that if they wish to take another partner (either marry one or live de facto) the resident could be legally forced by some of the more mercenary retirement village operators (courtesy of the Queensland Retirement Villages Act 1999) to sell his/her property, pay the exit fee and then have to buy back their own property at whatever amount is determined by the retirement village operators with, in some cases, an increased exit fee for the next sale? Most elderly residents simply can't afford to do that, so are robbed of living with a life partner during their twilight years. Shame on you Australia (and the Queensland Retirement Village Act) for allowing this travesty to continue.

Best regards,

Roberta Cava

25 March, (Tuesday) 9:28pm

Hi Roberta,

Herewith copy of the email I sent to Les Armstrong tonight. I hope they get their finger out and come up with a plan of attack.

We will need to get together with all correspondence to make a water-tight case if the media get involved. Channel Nine were asking for emails to expose injustices tonight on the 'Extra' program, but we would need to be sure of our facts ... the correspondence to date should help, so keep your letters. The media attack should have the support of ARQRV and come as a complete surprise to ACML. I pray that Les has the guts to fully support us, but I feel he may not be feeding all facts to the solicitor.

Hopefully he will respond this week.

Cheers Martin

25 March, (Tuesday) 9:12 pm

Hi Les,

I hope you had a good Easter break.

I am forwarding two letters relating to Roberta Cava and Meridien Lifestyles that David Wise may like to see as it confirms our fears that it is a waste of time my writing a letter to the CEO of ACML asking him to mediate. It's a closed shop!!

In the response from the Meridien Lifestyles CEO, Glen Brown, I am appalled when he states in his final paragraph that 'I have fully reviewed the results of these investigations and confirm that ACML staff involved have acted appropriately and that our decision to withdraw the previous offer stands' How can he review a situation without approaching both parties involved? What chance does any individual have when dealing with such an unfair and arrogant attitude. I pray that the solicitors of ARQRV know the answer. Do we have a case we can fight?

Regards

Martin Williams

March 27, (Thursday) 10:22 am

Hi Martin,

As I mentioned yesterday, it might be time for you to contact the lawyer directly to see what he is doing for us and have a list handy of all the questions we need answered. Here's a few I think should be asked:

1. What specifically can we charge them with: your loss of civil liberties; me with defamation of character/slander?
2. Is a 'guest licence' legal – it's not mentioned in the Retirement Village Act.
3. Is there any use at this time of sending your letter to the CEO of Meridien after the response we got from him?
4. Can they stop me from running my business from your unit?
5. What's the next step?
6. Should we go to the media now or after the tribunal?
7. Will they represent us, or do we have to get another lawyer to do that (is he too busy?)

I hope you can get some answers from the lawyer – because it sounds as if Les is foot-dragging. I know they are busy, but they can at least let us know what we should do about it. Love, R.

27 March, (Thursday) 12:43 pm

Hi Roberta,

I have not been able to find the business address and telephone number for David Wise, but do have his email so am preparing a letter to send ... copy to you. Love, M.

28 March, (Friday) – I went to the Master Chef dinner at the Leisure Centre with Martin. Again he was one of the chefs – great meals.

31 March – safety electrical switch installed in my unit

31 March, (Monday)

Hi Martin,

Lots of things have happened today:

Babette called: She and Doug are having a great time caravanning and have had many good experiences along the way - have made new friends and have had a lot of fun.

I've booked my flights to Canada – I leave for Singapore on 23 June - get back to Australia on July 22.

An electrician hired by L.J. Hooker came today and installed my electrical power switch – no charge to me.

Can you write to Meridien to determine from them how much it would cost for you to sell your property? Not to sell and re-buy - but to just sell it? And how much they would charge if you re-bought the property yourself. I think that information would be important information to have on file. Love you. R.

31 March, 10:39 pm

Hi Roberta,

Not until I have a definitive answer from David Wise. I do not want to give Michelle a whiff that I could be moving out at this stage. The vibes from ARQRV at the moment are to consider asking what would be the cost of selling and buying back my villa ... not a viable option in my opinion.

I have obtained a copy of the Current Title Search Wellington Manor Pty Ltd showing all residents, Record of Death and Transfer of new partner onto the lease for Bittel, Moxey and Riemers. I now need to try and obtain copies of their signed Title Form to send to David White as this will show a precedence within the Manor Group purchased by Meridien.

It looks as if John is too busy to go on holiday with Lorna this year so she will probably go on her own to the UK to visit family. I find that a great shame as it was important to Lorna to show England off to John and let him meet her family. It all seems to be one way at the moment with his family being forced onto Lorna.

Glad you had the power switch done at last. Love, M.

CHAPTER 10
APRIL, 2008

1 April, 2008, (Tuesday) – I went to Martin's tonight to attend a 76th birthday party for one of the fellows in the Master Chef team - Kevin. It was a lovely evening. Kevin's wife Marie also stated that the party was supposed to be a 'welcome to the village' party for me and expressed how unhappy she was that it hadn't happened.

The meal was lovely and the company was really great (14 people). A few of them were talking about getting the people in the village to sign a petition complaining that I had not been allowed to live there – not sure whether they will go ahead with it or not – time will tell.

[A petition was never done, but it could have made a tremendous difference to the outcome. As I said in the introduction: *'The world suffers a lot, not because of the actions of bad people but because of the silence of good people!'*]

Martin surprised me by giving me more flowers. This was lovely little turquoise and purple orchids. He is being very loving lately and keeps saying how sorry he is that we're having to go through this (as if it was his fault!). I keep trying to reassure him, but he doesn't seem to be reassured.

We have been told that the lawyer will get back to us on Friday. I stayed at Martin's overnight.

3 April, (Thursday)

Hi Martin,

I've heard from Martin, Sue, Michele, Helen and Pat and my schedule for my June/July Canada trip is A-okay with them - so I just have to book my flight from Kelowna to Calgary. Every time I go onto the internet Air Canada gives me a different fare, so think they are converting it to Aussie $ which is fluctuating now. Will still wait a little bit and keep checking because they often have seat sales that are really good.

Helen says she will either drive me to Edmonton on July 3rd (her son's birthday is on July 4th so she often drives there to be with him). If she can't drive me - there's a Red Arrow Bus that can drop me off near Mike's home. If he can't pick me up Patti has offered to do so - so everyone is co-operating and making it easy for me this trip.

I sent my travel info to several people in Winnipeg - 2 cousins, my best friend Pat and a few other friends - all have replied - except my son Brian.

Talk to you later.

Cheers, R.

3 April, (Thursday) 9:29pm

To: Bill Bittel (the man who was allowed to bring his partner into his home without all the fuss and bother we would have had to deal with.)

From: Martin

Les Armstrong of ARQRV, has said that their legal fellow is looking at my problem of Roberta being denied moving into my villa and requires a precedence of other occasions where residents of this village have remarried and brought their new spouse/partner into the village. The solicitor feels that he can argue the case if he can prove that the previous owners allowed this to happen by means of a solicitor adding the new spouse name to the Title. His argument being that when Meridien purchased Wellington Manor, they would have signed an agreement not to change the existing owners' procedures.

The question is; would you be prepared to provide a copy of the document showing the Queensland Titles Office acceptance of Brenda's transfer to your Lease?

I fully appreciate that this is an invasion of your privacy, but hearsay is not acceptable for yourself, Ron Poole and Alan Reimers, hence my request. I will not be offended if you refuse

Regards

Martin

5 April, (Saturday) – I had dinner at Martin's and stayed overnight (After Martin reported the event to 'mother' of course.)

6 April, (Sunday) – I had brekkie at the Leisure Centre with Martin.

6 April, (Sunday)

Hi Roberta

The following letter was received by your Association in July, 2006:

Below it you will find our answer - which was sent to the management of Wellington Manor Pty Ltd

28 July 2006 *17

The Directors
Wellington Manor Pty. Ltd.
269 Birkdale Rd.
Qld. 4159

Dear Sirs,

It is not evident to me that you have had a copy of McCullough Robertson's letter of 18 July addressed to me, so I enclose a copy. We have to assume of course that you are at least aware of its purport, which is an attempt to intimidate this Association, just as letters to the two applicants are similarly intimidatory.

This Association was very well aware, from the very beginning, of the case which residents of Wellington Manor brought against you and indeed was instrumental in its preparation. We knew all the circumstances, how the surpluses were accumulated, how much was involved and what issues were canvassed etc. In short we were fully informed of all aspects well before even the Section 154 meeting was sought. We needed subsequently to make no Einsteinian calculations to know what settlement entailed for the residents of Wellington Manor.

We shall not be offering any retraction or apology because there is nothing which we need to retract or for which we need apologise. If you can point to any error of fact or figure we will certainly publish a correction. Your practice of accumulating surpluses was a malpractice such as we shall always seek to expose. And, as you will be well aware, what you conceded at mediation could have been made an order of the Tribunal and was no more than the Commercial and Consumer Tribunal would undoubtedly have ordered had you persisted in defending your actions.

It would be in the better interests of the retirement village industry as a whole and all retirement village residents including, perhaps especially including, those of the Manor group of villages, if you were to refrain from trying to intimidate residents or this, their Association. You should, instead, devote yourselves much more assiduously to espousing the objects of the Retirement Villages Act as set out in Section 3 of the Act, particularly subsection (2)(a).

Yours faithfully

Phil Phillips

6 April, (Sunday) 4:35 pm

Subject: Intimidation

Hi Martin,

Were you aware of this information that is on the ARQRV website that must have accounted for the above reply?

Cheers, R.

18 July, 2006 *[18]

Mr. Phil Phillips, President
ARQRV
10 Edenlea Village
Townsend Qld 4556

Dear Mr. Phillips

WELLINGTON MANOR PTYT LTD – DEFAMATION

We act for Wellington Manor Pty Ltd and refer to the Association of Residents of Queensland Retire Villages Inc (ARQRV) Newsletter 58. The Newsletter contains allegations about our client that are both factually incorrect and defamatory.

These allegations are actionable under the tort of injurious falsehood, which entitles a corporation to recover damages for loss of business reputation arising from a defamatory publication. We refer you to the case of *Ratcliffe v Evans* [1892] 2 QB 524 and *Mirror Newspapers Ltd v World Hosts Pty Ltd* (1979) 141 CLR 632.Stadhams on 26 April 2006. This Deed contains a clause which requires the parties to keep the terms of the settlement confidential.

The Newsletter article publishes the substantive parts of the settlement thereby causing Messrs Kirk and Stradhams to breach this clause. It therefore gives rise to a right on the part of our client to sue under the tort of interference with the performance of a contract; in this regard see *Trade Practices Act* 1974 (Cth) (The TPA) which prohibits misleading and deceptive conduct in trade or commerce. This provision is given application to individuals with non-corporate entities in the event of publication by post by virtue of section 6. The Newsletter was sent by post; you therefore fall within the ambit of section 52 of the TPA and are potentially liable under that provision.

Our client's preference is to resolve this dispute without recourse to the Courts. In this regard, we are instructed that a front-page story in the next edition of the 'ARQRV Newsletter retracting the story complained of, along with a letter to our client apologising for the inaccurate and defamatory publication and undertaking never to publish inaccurate information regarding our client or any of its officers, employees or related companies again, will be an appropriate remedy.

If these terms are not acceptable, we hold instructions to vigorously protect our client's reputation.

We also put you on notice that our client will also be seeking remedies against the other committee members.

Could we please have your response to the letter by close of business on Monday 24 July, 2006.

Yours faithfully

Bill Manning

McCullough Robertson

I think I have a strong case to show that they have tarnished both my personal and professional image by refusing to let me move in with you – as if I were a criminal.

Love, R

6 April, (Sunday)

I was aware of that one against the original owners. Shortly after that all residents received a substantial rebate of around $700 as a result of the Tribunal ruling.

L Martin

It was shortly after this that Martin and I had a conversation, where I strongly suggested that we hire a lawyer to sue Michelle Smith and Meridien for intimidation, slander and defamation of character. Not only did she bar me from residing in the village but she insinuated that I was an unsavoury person. To my knowledge, the only people that could be barred from the village would be those under 50 years of age, had a criminal record or were unsavoury criminals. By barring me, she also put a black mark on my company Cava Consulting insinuating that the owner was a criminal or worse.

Martin refused to take this step – said I would have to do it on my own. So, rather than go against his wishes, I tried to think of another way we could get Meridien to change their mind and let me reside in the village. I was constantly aware that three months had already gone by and the lease for my unit was for six months – that left us only three months to settle the issue. It didn't seem that ARQRV were doing much to settle the issue either.

8 April, (Tuesday)

Hi Martin,

Jann Stuckey was one of the first people I met after I immigrated to Australia. At that time she owned a training firm and I offered seminars through her firm for the first year I lived here. So I thought I would see if she could help us out especially since she represented the portfolio of the Fair trading when the Retirement Villages Amendment Bill was tabled in parliament in 2006.

Let me know what you think of the information I sent her.

Cheers, R.

Here's the information from the Weekly Hansard:

51st Parliament [19]

Tuesday, 28 February 2006

RETIREMENT VILLAGES AMENDMENT BILL

Second Reading

Resumed from 14 February 2006 (see p. 46)

Mrs STUCKEY (Currumbin—Lib) (5.18 pm): I rise today to speak on the Retirement Villages Amendment Bill 2006 in my capacity as shadow minister for tourism, fair trading and wine industry development. I wish to inform the House that I myself am the owner of a unit, albeit for holiday letting, and am hereby declaring this interest.

I thank the minister for agreeing to a hurried briefing on this bill from her departmental staff just prior to today's debate - a briefing at short notice because this bill was only tabled in the House on 14 February 2006. In relation to this bill I would like to take a few moments to advise the House of recent figures released in the Productivity Commission report on the economic implications of an ageing

Australia which stated that one in four Australians would be 65 plus by 2044-45. We already have 2.5 million Australians over this age and with the retirement population expected to double during the next 25 years it is no wonder the issue of retirement villages is one which needs to be addressed sooner rather than later.

The Retirement Villages Amendment Bill 2006, the bill, amends the Retirement Villages Act 1999, the act, and seeks to clarify the rights and obligations of residents and operators, make the operator's budget decisions more transparent and accountable, streamline access to the dispute resolution process and offer greater certainty of a resident's financial liability. The act, which commenced on 1 July 2000, regulates the retirement village industry which in Queensland comprises more than 250 registered retirement village schemes, providing the accommodation, social and recreational needs of persons 55 years and over.

In the Currumbin electorate 38 per cent of registered voters are eligible to live in a retirement village. Retirement villages are popular in that they provide a degree of security. Residents are in a mature age bracket, there are no noisy children or teenagers, property is looked after when away and there is minimal maintenance.

There are numerous circumstances which have to be taken into account when addressing the needs of those in retirement villages. Residents may acquire freehold title to the unit or be granted a lease or licence over the unit. In return for an ingoing contribution and entering into a residence contract, persons obtain a right to reside in the village and receive services. Residents then pay ongoing general services charges which are used to maintain the village capital items and cover recurrent village expenses.

One of the significant initiatives of the act was the creation of the maintenance reserve fund and the capital replacement fund which accorded increased accountability in dealing with village expenditure. However, I remind the House that when the act was introduced the then Labor minister gave an undertaking to review the effectiveness of the act after its first year of operation. This review of the act commenced in September 2001, but it was not until 23 February 2005 that a draft bill was released—that is nearly 3½ years later. Like a broken record we hear time and again from Labor ministers that they are undertaking reviews yet the results of these reviews do not see the light of day until several years down the track.

Most of the key policy objectives of the bill, which is designed to reinforce fair trading principles, are worthy of mention. These include clause 4, which aims to regulate and promote fair trading practices in the operation of retirement villages and focuses on consumer protection. Whilst it is heartening to see a genuine recognition of consumer protection, it is a sad indictment of previous caretakers of this portfolio when the current minister admits consumer protection had not been a focus of the Office of Fair Trading. Also included is a clarification of voting rights, particularly for residents unable to attend a meeting; easier access to the dispute resolution tribunal for residents who are too elderly or intimidated to pursue this process themselves; the involvement of residents in the village budget setting process; greater disclosure of financial information; <u>and limited rights for a spouse or relative to continue living in the unit should the resident die or vacate the unit, even if not a party to the residency contract.</u>

Not so palpable, though, are some stricter guidelines for increasing fees and charges; clarification of work involving reinstating a unit to focus more on ensuring a swift resale; and the cessation of a resident's liability to pay fees and charges after vacation if their vacated unit remains unsold after nine months. In essence, the majority of issues relating to retirement villages which arise on a regular basis are based around a number of vital areas and include: fees, incorporating entry fees; ongoing maintenance fees and deferred management fees; the village rules, including voting rights at meetings, visitors, pets, noise and adjustment to structures; and the control of transfer or sale of units with particular reference to delays with sales, fees associated with sales and the price achieved.

Society today views retirement villages as being an integral and valuable component of community life and quite rightly so. Undoubtedly as our population lives longer and Queensland continues to be a desirable location, aged-care facilities will prosper throughout our region. I am sure most members in this House contributing to this debate will agree that <u>fairness and equity for residents and operators alike</u> must be paramount. By acknowledging these moral principles we must be careful not to impinge on the commercial realities associated with this accommodation sector. After all they need to remain economically viable to be able to maintain standards of health, safety and comfort.

Adequate regulation of villages where the residents own the freehold title to their units and the recognition of the role of the body corporate to facilitate equitable treatment in such villages are issues that require ongoing attention. Legislative changes have been made to residency contracts entered into prior to the act to bring them in line with post act contracts. In fact there are four proposed amendments reflected in clauses 8, 23, 26 and 44, which will have a retrospective effect, applying to and affecting contracts on foot, yet they will not affect rights as they existed prior to the commencement of this act.

Discussion with industry stakeholders brought forward several reservations that these clauses may present some confusion for residents and operators who may not fully understand the ramifications of this retrospectivity. Of particular note was the fact that these clauses were also raised by the Scrutiny of Legislation Committee as having the potential to impact adversely on retirement home operators. The committee has referred to parliament the question of whether these retrospective provisions have sufficient regard to the rights of retirement home operators.

[The Queensland Retirement Village Act 1999 is still in force, so none of the above recommendations were adopted and the Act remains the same.]

8 April, (Tuesday) 3:56 pm

To: Jann Stuckey
Subject: Retirement Villages

Hi Jann,

I was doing some research on the net about retirement village Schemes and came across your enclosed comments regarding the Retirement Villages Amendment Bill. Because you have obviously done considerable research on the topic of Retirement Villages, I'm taking the liberty of asking your advice (not official mind you) about a situation I have faced recently regarding a retirement village in Birkdale (Redlands district – yes I know I could contact Mr. English). At this time I am hoping that the ARQRV's lawyer will be able to come up with something, and it is taking some time to get advice on how we should proceed after this point.

One thing not covered in the Retirement Village Act is what would happen if one of the couple die, and the remaining person wants to have a new partner move in with them. They can run into all kinds of problems. For example – here's what happened to me:

Martin and his wife decided to move to Australia from England so they could spend their retirement years closer to their daughter

Lorna and her family. So in 2001 they came to Queensland and bought a property. Soon, though they realised how lonely they were and started looking into the advantages and disadvantages of living in a retirement village. So they bought a lovely three-bedroom villa in Wellington Manor, a large retirement village in Birkdale, Queensland that was still under construction.

Because Martin could not work in Australia, he used his considerable amount of energy to set up an association for the village owners. He was soon the president of their association and became one of the many forward-thinking members of a committee to set things up so that the owners would really enjoy living in their village. Soon there were five core men who started a once-a-month 'master chef' night where they cooked a two-course gourmet treat – then a 'Sunday Brekkie' of bacon and eggs where the men did all the cooking. These became favourite times. Then the 'Happy Hour' on Friday nights was started, Western film night, bowls, croquet and many other sporting activities were arranged. It was a happy time for the village owners and a fun place to live.

Life did not turn out like Martin planned though, and his lovely wife was stricken and died of cancer in late 2004. The village rallied and did their best to help Martin through his bereavement. When his wife first became ill, Martin had to stop much of his volunteer work, but slowly but surely he pitched in and began living life again.

However, he was lonely, and started seeking female companionship. In early 2007 he met me and we started dating. However, because I lived over one hundred kilometres away, it was difficult. We finally decided to spend alternate weekends at each other's homes. Then we took a one month holiday to North America and found we got along very well – so much so that in December of last year we decided that when my lease ran out on February 11th, that we would move in together.

After discussing several alternatives about where we could live, we came to the conclusion that Martin would lose far too much equity in his property for him to sell his unit. You see, his contract with the retirement village owners stated that he would have to pay an exit fee of 30% of the current value of his property plus 50% of the increase in value of his property, refurbishment costs of replacing his white goods and real estate fees. He realised that he would lose approximately half the value of his unit that was worth approximately $500,000. He realised that with only approximately $250,000 left he wouldn't have enough to purchase another comparable home. Besides, he loved living there, the residents welcomed me with open arms and I found the residents up-beat and happy people. So I agreed to move in with him.

I gave notice that I would be vacating my rental home on the Gold Coast on February 11th. I would bring approximately half of my belongings to Martin's and store the rest. Martin sold some of his furniture to make room for my furniture.

Until April of 2007, Martin's retirement village was run very successfully by the Manor Group, but was bought out by Meridien who were gobbling up retirement villages at an amazing rate. The village association had been assured by Meridien that everything would remain the same for the village owners. However, this is not what is happening, and the association is constantly battling with the new owners to live up to their promise that 'nothing would change.'

In mid-December, Martin contacted Meridien to advise them that I was going to move in with him and was advised that he had three options:

1. If he wanted me to be part owner of the property, he would have to sell his property, pay the exit fee, and buy it back at whatever value given by the retirement village operators. (Not a viable option).

2. I would have to sign a 3-page 'Long Term Guest Licence' that allowed me to live with Martin. We would have to pay $700 for this licence. [There is no mention of such a licence in the Retirement Villages Act of 1999 in Queensland.] This was accompanied by an 11-page car parking licence and that I would have pay $50 per month for parking.

3. I could stay for three weeks, leave the village for one day and repeat the process.

None of these options were fully acceptable to us. The first option was met with open-mouthed amazement that the owners could have the gall to suggest it. It stated:

'As previously advised, should Ms Cava wish to be considered a resident for the purposes of the Act, then the existing residence contract that you have entered into would need to be terminated and

a new residence contract (in your name and Ms Cava's name) would need to be entered into. Of course, this will trigger payment of any exit fees under your current residence contract, the issue of a new Public Information document to both parties and the payment of a new ingoing contribution.'

This new PID (Public Information Document) would have a maximum exit fee of 36% - not the 30% fee that is in Martin's existing document. Martin and I decided that option was out of the question not only because it appeared unfair, but because it also appeared to be a case of 'double-dipping' of exit fees. Besides, Martin couldn't afford to lose 50% of his equity in his home.

Martin pointed out to the Operator that other residents in the village had re-married and that the Manor Group had directed their lawyers to add the new partner as a village resident paying just the normal legal fees to change the document without adding (in some cases), their partner to the Public Information Document. They did not have to sell and re-buy their own properties as we were told we had to do.

We asked to see a copy of the second option – the 'Long Term Guest Licence.' No one in the village had heard of such a thing. When the document was delivered in mid-December, Meridien encouraged us to take the three-page document to a lawyer. We did so, but couldn't get an appointment till the second week in December. Our lawyer asked us who had prepared the document. There were so many errors and omissions in it that he suggested that it had been thrown together by a legal clerk – certainly not by a qualified lawyer. The lawyer advised that any agreement signed by the resident, guest and owners was in fact a contract, and not a licence, to allow relatives, carer's etc., to move into the retirement village and be free to use the village facilities. He promptly advised us to remove two clauses because they absolved the Operators of their 'Duty of Care' responsibilities:

'Releases the Operator from all liability (whether in contract, tort, by statute or otherwise however) in respect of all claims whatever relating to, the use and occupation of the Unit by the Guest and the residing within the Village by the Guest.'

'The Guest releases and indemnifies the Operator and agrees to keep the Operator and its employees, agents and contractors released and at all times indemnified to the fullest extent permitted

by law from and against all claims of every description whatever incurred by the Operator or for which the Operator may be or become liable whether in contract, tort, by statute or otherwise however and during or after the term of the Licence in respect of or arising from, the use and occupation of the Unit by the Guest and the residing in the Village by the Guest.'

The lawyer also advised that there was nothing in the contract protecting Martin, should our relationship break up, so he added a new item,

'The licence expires on the termination of the relationship of the guest and the resident.'

He also advised that because the licence was a template for many similar situations, there should be no charge to the resident. He also questioned the legal fee of $700 for a standard legal document that likely took about fifteen minutes to prepare (meaning the 'lawyer' would be earning approximately $2,800 per hour). In fact, because the document had to be re-written, he advised us that we should not be paying any legal fee charged by the Operator.

Because the third option (stay three weeks – out one day, etc.) seemed rather an absurd suggestion, it certainly would not be a viable option.

On Friday, January 18th, just one day before Martin and I were to take a planned two-week vacation to New Zealand, we took the revised Long Term Guest Licence to a Justice of the Peace and had it witnessed. That same day a meeting was held to give the signed document to Ms Michelle Smith, General Manager, Queensland of the Meridien Management Group. She adamantly rejected the document and said it had to remain as it was except for the addition of the extra clause relating to their relationship breaking up. A heated argument took place after which Ms Smith threatened to remove the Guest licence. I gathered our documents together and stormed out of the meeting. Before Martin left the meeting, he stated that he would get the document to our lawyer, but because we were leaving on holiday the next day, we could not have the document signed again by a Justice of the Peace until we returned on February 4th.

When I checked my mail upon my return from NZ, I saw that the lawyer had adapted the document to suit Meridien. Martin also received a letter from Ms. Smith. We were flabbergasted to find it stated that Meridien were formally withdrawing their offer of a Long Term Guest Licence due to my 'attitude to retirement living.' She also objected to my use of profanity (I used the words 'that stinks' and 'crap' to describe my opinion of option number one - a view taken by virtually everyone in the village we spoke to later).

She dumped this disastrous news on us one week before the removalists were coming to collect my belongings. We just sat there looking at each other thinking, 'What are we going to do?' Martin decided he would attempt to get Ms Smith to reconsider the contents of her letter. He left two telephone calls for her, which she finally answered at noon on Wednesday and stated that even if he were to marry me, I would not be allowed to move into his home.

With five days left till my planned move, I began frantically searching for a new home close to where Martin lived. Luckily, on Thursday I found a unit and was able to move in four days later on February 11th. Because we cannot share expenses as planned, this adds over $1,400 per month to my expenses.

You can imagine what we have gone through since that time and wonder if you have any suggestions as to how we can deal with this obvious discrimination by a retirement village operator.

I hope you can help.

Roberta Cava

8 April, (Tuesday) 4:05 pm

From: Currumbin Electorate Office
Subject: Retirement Villages

Good afternoon

As Jann is no longer Shadow Minister for Fair Trading, she does not have responsibility for these issues. I am happy to forward your email onto Mr Mark McArdle MP, Shadow Attorney-General and Shadow Minister for Justice and Fair Trading, who now has responsibility in that area.

Please advise if you would like us to take this course of action.

Regards

Bev Malseed
Electorate Officer for
Jann Stuckey MP
Shadow Minister for Child Safety and Women

I asked her to send the info to the new minister, but have never received a reply. [Another dead end!]

9 April, (Wednesday) 10:29 am

Subject: Permission

Hello Les,

Martin Williams has been telling me about what you are doing about our situation with Meridien. Hopefully David Wise will get back to us soon with some kind of resolution to our situation.

In the meantime, I'm pleased that you're interested in helping me with the research for a book I have tentatively named *'Dealing with Retirement Village Bullies – Think before you buy!* To write it, I will need your help in obtaining the following:

- I would need formal written permission from the ARQRV (on your stationary) to use the information in your newsletters and any other material you might suggest using relating to the problems faced by residents. Your association, of course, would obtain credit for allowing me to use that information in the book.
- Can you reveal the reasons for past tribunals in Queensland and what the resolutions were for those cases?
- How many were settled at a tribunal – out of court?
- Who are the major retirement village operators in Queensland that seem to be causing the most difficulties to residents?
- A list of the contact people in the other states and/or federal associations that assist seniors in retirement villages. It would help to know whether they also have regular newsletters they send to their membership.

I would like to meet you one time when you're in the area – or Martin and I could make a trip to your retirement village if that is more convenient for you.

Best regards, Roberta Cava

[Unfortunately the above information was never sent to me.]

10 April, (Thursday)

Hi Martin,

Thought you might be interested in what Mr Rogers had to say about removal of village managers in the Hansard Report for Tuesday February 28th, 2006. It might be worth investigating ...

[20] Mr ROGERS (Redcliffe—Lib) (5.44 pm): I rise to speak to the Retirement Villages Amendment Bill. Why is Redcliffe a retirement mecca? If it were not for retirement in Redcliffe I would not have met my wife when her parents retired there. Redcliffe has several retirement villages. In my days as an accountant I audited the bodies corporate of some and I met the people who lived there. Their passion for their village is tremendous.

I have only two issues with this bill—and I am going to try to keep it short—and one is retrospectivity. I do not believe in retrospective legislation. I believe it is unjust and unfair because people plan their lives based on the legislation at the time. To then come out and say, 'No, we have changed our mind. We are going to change the law,' is unfair and unjust for all those concerned. People cannot plan if the government is going to retrospectively change the laws after they have been enacted.

Clauses 8, 23, 26 and 44 have retrospective application and these should not be included.

The other issue is the imposition on the operators to provide their financial statements to the people of the retirement villages. People do not go to a corner store or the fish and chips shop and say, 'Before I'm going to buy lunch, show me your financial statements.' That is just not on. It is not a commercial act and that provision should not be included, either. Yet again, it is unfair on the commercial operators of any business to have to disclose how they operate their business and their financial position. <u>If the retirement village is working well, the people in the park will be happy to deal with them. If not, they can remove the management of the village. I have been involved in retirement villages where the management has been removed.</u>

As I said, I did not intend to speak to this bill for very long. In fact, I have a whole minute up so far. My points are: do not disclose the financial statements of the operators and retrospective legislation is unfair and unjust. My final comment, as members have come to learn, is Redcliffe is a retirement mecca. Why? People have gone there for a variety of reasons: the sea, the community atmosphere, the shopping facilities. The one thing they have not come for is the rail line to Redcliffe. We do not have a rail line to Redcliffe, and the people in our retirement villages would appreciate it.

10 April, (Thursday) 4:16 pm

Hi sweetie,

I'll speak to you later about the Hansard article

Love, Martin

Letter sent to residents by the CEO of AMP Capital Meridien Lifestyle, Glen Brown

10 April, 2008 *21

Dear Resident

As a valued resident of Wellington Manor, we would like to inform you of some recent developments.

The joint venture partners in AMP Capital Meridien Lifestyle ('ACML'), Meridien Retirement Living and AMP Capital Investors, will soon announce that they have commenced a strategic review of options for their portfolio of Villages currently owned and operated within Australia.

We believe we have made significant progress in a range of options including the introduction of new investors for the business to assist in enhancing future growth and improvements in our existing retirement communities.

We have appointed Caliburn Partnership to assist with this review.

It is 'business as usual' for our residents and employees and we retain our ongoing focus to deliver the highest standard of retirement living to you – our residents.

I would also reiterate that the most valuable assets in the business remain our people – our residents and staff. We look forward to continuing to improve our on-going service to you

Yours faithfully,

Glen Brown – Chief Executive Officer
AMP Capital Meridien Lifestyle

10 April, (Thursday) 4:29pm

Hi,

How are you today? I almost asked you for dinner tonight, but realised that I had put out chicken liver - and I don't think you really like liver do you? If you're interested let me know and come on over. I still have some of your red wine here too. You don't have to stay the night, just come for dinner?

What say you? Love, R.

11 April, Friday – I attended the Ladies Probus meeting.

12 April, (Saturday) – I went with Martin to luncheon to celebrate a resident's 70th birthday (the Justice of the Peace who notarised our Long Term Guest Licence).

12 April

Hi Martin,

I found the following article in the Australia Financial Review re: Property

AMP-Meridien [22]

Ben Wilmot

An expected split of the $1 billion joint venture between AMP Capital Investors and the private Meridien Group could kick off a new round of consolidation in the retirement industry.

The pair have appointed investment bank Caliburn Partner-ship to conduct a strategic review of their AMP Capital Meridien Lifestyle joint venture. Observers are tipping that the entire portfolio could come to the market in coming months.

A full or partial sale would be the largest offering in the Australian retirement sector and the outcome of the review could shape the future of the sector over the next five years.

The portfolio is about 50 per cent larger than the Zig Inge portfolio that sold for $641 million last year, and is considered a standout because of the difficulty in replicating the business, which spans Queensland, NSW and South Australia.

The 25-strong portfolio of retirement villages comes with a solid development pipeline and will pit major property groups against

invest-ment banks and even sovereign funds interested in the sector.

Industry players are tipping a split between AMP and Meridien even though they teamed up just 12 months ago, when the funds management giant backed the small private group's purchases across the sector.

Over the past two years, Meridien has bought the four-strong Glen Group portfolio in NSW, the nine- strong Gannon Estates portfolio in SA and NSW, two Manor Group retirement villages in Queensland and a swag of individual villages.

The group's portfolio is now one of the largest in Australia and comprises four villages in Queensland, nine in NSW and 12 in SA.

It includes 2864 independent living units and 467 serviced apartments. The group has approval for another 515 units and 102 apartments, to be delivered over the next five years.

All the villages in the portfolio are wholly owned by the joint venture and use modern deferred management fee structures.

The Brisbane-based management platform is one of the best-regarded in the market and includes a host of former FKP executives.

Large property players are expected to chase the portfolio because of its scale and geographic diversity. Other major portfolios that have changed hands recently have been focused on single states, especially Victoria.

Although the joint venture has released little financial information, the group's villages are said to be recording good price growth on unit resales.

Caliburn is believed to have been called in as AMP and Meridien have split on how quickly they want to grow. Their views on capital expenditure are also believed to have diverged.

Possibilities to be considered include Meridien aligning with another partner for all or part of the portfolio, introducing a new investor to the joint venture, or even selling out.

A full-scale sale will only be pursued if there is sufficient demand, most likely from potential trade buyers, as the uncertain equities market would make a float unlikely.

Industry observers said AMP Capital Investors could be inclined to step back from the venture, while Meridien was likely to continue as operator of the portfolio of villages.

KEY POINTS

- *The 25-strong portfolio of villages has a solid development pipeline.*
- *All the villages are wholly owned by the joint venture.*

515 units and 102 apartments, to be delivered over the next five years.

All the villages in the portfolio are wholly owned by the joint venture and use modern deferred management fee structures.

The Brisbane-based management platform is one of the best-regarded in the market and includes a host of former FKP executives.

Large property players are expected to chase the portfolio because of its scale and geographic diversity. Other major portfolios that have changed hands recently have been focused on single states, especially Victoria.

Although the joint venture has released little financial information, the group's villages are said to be recording good price growth on unit resales.

Caliburn is believed to have been called in as AMP and Meridien have split on how quickly they want to grow. Their views on capital expenditure are also believed to have diverged. Possibilities to be considered include Meridien aligning with another partner for all or part of the portfolio, introducing a new investor to the joint venture, or even selling out. A full-scale sale will only be pursued if there is sufficient demand, most likely from potential trade buyers, as the uncertain equities market would make a float unlikely. Industry observers said AMP Capital Investors could be inclined to step back from the venture, while Meridien was likely to continue as operator of the portfolio of villages.

So, it looks as if Meridien and AMP are splitting up. Could it be because of the methods Meridien take in being Operators of their Retirement Villages?

19 April, (Saturday) – Martin and I and a group from the village went to a theatre to see *Mid-Life Crisis*. It was an excellent night – lots of laughs.

25 April, (Friday) 9:24 am

Hi Martin,

This morning I decided to put something together to send to the CEO of AMP.

Shame on you for passing the buck to Glen Brown the CEO of Meridien to investigate our situation. It's obvious that he carefully interviewed both Ms. Diane Brown and Ms Michelle Smith, but did not have the courtesy to speak to either Mr. Martin Williams or myself. It's now clear to me who is setting the guidelines followed by Meridien employees responsible for handling situations at the Wellington Manor Retirement Village.

I've now had written confirmation that AMP and Meridien concentrates its importance in the almighty dollar – not in doing what is best for retirement village seniors.

However, don't think I will take the time to write to someone that will ignore my letter ... so you're the only one that will read it.

Cheers, R.

26 April, (Saturday) – 50th anniversary dinner at village for Brian and Angela.

27 April, (Sunday) 5:44 pm

Hi Martin,

I spoke with Alex Thomson, the wife of the journalist Tuck Thomson with the Courier Mail. She suggested that I call him tomorrow at the Courier Mail office in Brisbane.

We should decide what we will say. I think we will need a ball-park figure of what you would lose if you were forced to leave the village so we could live together. To my recollection it is as follows:

1. 30% of the present value of the property ($450,000 = $150,000.)

2. 50% of the capital again since you purchased the property in 2001 - (approx: $450,000 less $320,000 = 230,000 gain X 50% = $115,000)

3. Real estate fees???

4. Refurbishment?

5. Other fees?

We also should establish how much per month we are losing because we are not able to share expenses. i.e. - your existing expenses plus any extras it would cost to have me living there ($50 parking fee etc.) plus what it is costing me per month to live in a separate home.

Maybe we should both put together something in writing that we could send to him after we speak with him.

What do you think?

Cheers, R.

(This was edited by us both before being sent on April 28th)

27 April, (Sunday) 9:12 pm

Hi Roberta,

Your figures are basically correct but, as it is a Meridien paper exercise, I would remain in the villa and there would be no refurbishment or estate agent charges ... there would however, be substantial lawyers' fees.

If the Courier mail is interested in following up the story, we would definitely provide accurate information and meet up with him, ideally at my villa so that he can get a good 'feel' for the story. Would he bring in the TV media for a bigger splash I wonder?

The point also needs to be made that we both decided not to include your name onto the lease and that there is no mechanism for this in the 'Act' ... hence the legally dubious Long Term Licence Agreement with all of its limitations to your freedom and protection.

Brenda rang me earlier today and left a message about the article in today's Sunday Mail on page 18 about seniors moving in together to help make ends meet in the current pinch on pensions and CPI.

I have to go out a 10 am tomorrow if you need to speak before contacting me.

Love M

27 April, (Sunday) 9:23 pm

I have just noticed that the capital gain is $130.000, (not $230.000) so $65.000 would be added to the $150.000 giving a total loss of

$215.000 to sell and re-purchase my home, plus solicitors fees and other incidentals of removalists and storage etc.

Love M

27 April, (Sunday) 9:57 pm

Hi Martin,

I missed that article in the Sunday Mail and it has gone out with my recycling stuff. Would you please send me a copy of the article?

I think the media need to know what it would cost you because I'm not allowed to move in with you. There are not many options Meridien have left open to us - so it would appear that you would have to move out so we could live together. That's why I needed those figures. I know it would not be as much if they allowed me to be put on the title - but they have not allowed that option.

Love, R.

28 April, (Monday)

Hi again,

Here is the front page of the fax I sent to AMP and the information I have put together for the Courier Mail fellow.

Cheers, R.

After some editing with the help of Martin, I did send the following letter:

28 April 2008 (Monday) *[23]

AMP
33 Alfred Street
Sydney, NSW 2000

Attn: Craig Dunn, CEO

Re: Proposed Long Term Guest Licence – Villa 3196 Wellington Manor Retirement Village

I was disappointed to see that you passed the buck to Glen Brown the CEO of Meridien to investigate our situation. A full investigation did not take place. Apparently, Glen Brown interviewed both Ms. Diane Brown and Ms Michelle Smith, but did not have the courtesy to speak to either Mr. Martin Williams or myself. Although he stated in his letter *'I have fully reviewed the results of these investigations* and confirm that all ACML staff involved have acted appropriately and that our decision to withdraw the previous offer [Long Term Guest Licence] stands.' How can he state emphatically that he 'investigated' the issue fully?

It's now very clear who is setting the guidelines for Meridien employees responsible for handling situations at the Wellington Manor Retirement Village. His letter gives written confirmation that Meridien staff concentrate their attention on the almighty dollar – not on doing what is best for retirement village seniors.

I was pleased to read in the Australian Financial Review that you are seriously contemplating splitting from The Meridien Group. That will be a smart move on your part. I might even consider re-investing in AMP again if that does occur.

Sincerely,

Roberta Cava

28 April, (Monday) 5:02 pm

Subject: Courier Mail Submission (2nd draft)

Hi Roberta,

I have had a quick stab at editing and seem to have changed a lot in the early part re the build up of village facilities. I am not sure that any of this would be relevant to the Courier Mail ... they would certainly précis it to a few paragraphs, but the article as written does give a full background and explanation of events.

Anyway, read it through to see if it flows in the correct sequence.

Love, Martin

28 April (Monday)

Good Morning,

Thanks for correcting the information.

I'm thinking we should also go to the television stations and wonder whether you should do it or me. The contacts are as follows:

A Current Affair (Channel 9 news) (Tell us your story)

Today Tonight (Channel Seven News)

Let me know whether you want to contact them or should I?

Love, R.

29 April, (Tuesday) 10:26 am

Hi Martin,

I have changed the info for the Courier Mail as per enclosure. I've used most of your info, but have adapted others. I've written it in the 'third person' rather than using 'I, we and us' throughout the document.

Let me know whether you will be contacting the TV people.

Love, R.

29 April, 12:13 pm

Hi Roberta,

I find it rather difficult to read without spaces between the paragraphs and don't think the 'third person' report works very well in some areas. There is also a sentence with 'we' in it, so I think we should sit down together and go through each paragraph to ensure accuracy.

All mention of the Residents Association having problems with Meridien over changes should be removed because this is privileged information in the minutes of Committee meetings and not for general publication.

I note you have taken out the words 'it stinks' and 'crap' from your original draft! I think this is a very important point for us to bring up as it closes the door upon Meridien saying about the 'profanity' issue in their defence to the media. Let the readers be aware of how stupid it was for Michelle to use this as an excuse.

I am out at the men's club this afternoon so will contact you after Pool tonight.

Love M

29 April, 10:36 am

Hi Martin,

Because there isn't much space to 'tempt' the media on-line, I suggest that we say the following so they will investigate further:

'A resident who has lived in the Wellington Manor Retirement Village in Birkdale, Queensland since 2001, has asked for and been denied the right by their scheme operators (AMP Capital Meridien Lifestyle) to have a new partner move in with him. This decision was received one week before his partner's removalists were coming to move her in with him.'

What do you think of the wording?

Love, R.

Hi Roberta,

I have had a quick stab at editing and seem to have changed a lot in the early part re the build up of village facilities. I am not sure that any of this would be relevant to the Courier Mail ... they would certainly précis it to a few paragraphs, but the article as written does give a full background and explanation of events.

Anyway, read it through to see if it flows in the correct sequence.

Love, Martin

29 April, 12:11 pm

Hi Roberta,

I am not intending to do anything about a TV investigation until after Stanthorpe.

I don't know how many words you can submit to the media on-line, but I think the loss of Marguerite is an important factor for tugging the heartstrings. Suggest it is added as follows:

'A resident who has lived in the Wellington Manor Retirement Village in Birkdale, Queensland since 2001 and became a widower in 2004, has asked for and been denied the right by the scheme operators (AMP Capital Meridien Lifestyle) to have a new partner move in with him. This decision was received one week before his partner's removalists were coming to move her in with him.'

Love M

[I decided that if Martin wasn't going to contact the media, I would. So I contacted several newspapers, Channel 7 Today Tonight and Channel 9 Current Affairs. Shortly after receiving Martin's email I sent the media representatives the following message:]

'A resident who has lived in the Wellington Manor Retirement Village in Birkdale, Queensland since 2001 and became a widower in 2004, has asked for and been denied the right by the scheme operators (AMP Capital Meridien Lifestyle) to have a new partner move in with him. This decision was received one week before his partner's removalists were coming to move her in with him.'

29 April, 3:27 pm (from Today Tonight Channel 7)

Subject: Today Tonight

Hello

We have received your email regarding the retirement village.

Could you please call me in the office on (gave phone number)

Cheers

Karryn Cooper
Today Tonight

29 April, 4:57 pm

Subject: Today Tonight

Hello Karryn,

As requested, I've enclosed the information that gives more information about the problems my partner Martin and I have had with AMP Capital Meridien Lifestyle and their denying me the right to live with my partner in Wellington Manor in Birkdale, Queensland.

For more background on me, please look up my web page.

I will discuss doing an interview with Martin and look forward to speaking to you later (possibly tomorrow at 9:30 am.)

Best regards, Roberta Cava

[I enclosed the following final draft of information that both Martin and I had agreed upon.]

WILLIAMS & CAVA and AMP CAPITAL MERIDIEN LIFESTYLE
*24

This situation involves:

Martin Williams –resident of the Wellington Manor Retirement Village, Birkdale.

Roberta Cava -who wants to live with her partner Martin.

Michelle Smith – General Manager, Queensland for AMP Capital Meridien Lifestyle (ACML)

Diane Brown – ACML village Manager of Wellington Manor and Cleveland Manor

Glen Brown – CEO of AMP Capital Meridien Lifestyle (ACML)

Craig Dunn - CEO of AMP Capital Investors

One thing not covered in the Queensland Retirement Village Act, 1999 is what happens if one of the couple die, and the remaining person wants a new partner to move in with him/her. They can run into all kinds of problems. For example – here's what happened to Martin and Roberta.

Martin Williams and his wife Anita decided to move to Australia from England in 2001 using an Australian Immigration Aged Parent visa to spend their retirement years closer to their daughter and her family. They bought a lovely three-bedroom villa in Wellington Manor, a large retirement village in Birkdale, Queensland that was still under construction.

The eighty, or so, village residents at that time voted to become Wellington Manor Residents Association Inc. and in December 2001, Martin was elected President. For the next two years, Martin and the members of his committee expended a tremendous amount of time and energy in obtaining benefits and improvements from the then village owners, Manor Group Pty Ltd. The association encouraged residents and new arrivals into the village to organise regular sporting and social activities. The introduction of a weekly happy hour became a major social event. Now seven years later with a population of around 240 residents, the village is a vibrant and active community where volunteer residents organise a whole host of regular functions and activities.

In 2004, one enterprising resident organised a small group of male volunteers (of whom Martin is a member) to prepare and serve a two-course gourmet dinner at $5.00 a head for around 100 residents, this giving the ladies a night off. This has now been expanded to include fish and chips for a monthly film night, a Sunday Western and chow night, Trivia night and more recently, a bi-monthly Sunday brekkie. It was a happy time for the village residents and a fun place to live.

Martin's wife died in late 2004 after a long battle against cancer. The village residents rallied and did their best to help him through his bereavement. During the latter stages of his wife's illness, Martin resigned as President. He had to stop much of his volunteer work, but slowly but surely he pitched in and began living life again.

In early 2007 he met Roberta and they started dating. This was difficult because she lived over one hundred kilometres away. They finally decided to spend alternate weekends at each other's homes. Then they took a one month holiday to North America and found they got along very well – so much so that in December of 2007, they decided that when her lease ran out on February 11th, that they would move in together.

After discussing several alternatives about where they could live, they came to the conclusion that Martin would lose far too much equity in his property for him sell his unit. You see, his contract with the retirement village owners stated that he would have to pay an exit fee of 30% of the current value of his property plus 50% of the increase in value of his property, refurbishment costs and real estate fees. He realised that he would lose approximately half the value of his unit that was worth approximately $450,000 and knew that with only approximately $225,000 left he wouldn't have enough to purchase a comparable home. Besides, he loved living there. Roberta found the residents up-beat and happy people and they welcomed her with open arms, so she agreed to move in with Martin.

Until April of 2007, Martin's retirement village had been run very successfully by the Manor Group, but was bought out by AMP Capital Meridien Lifestyle (ACML) who gobbled up retirement villages at an amazing rate. The Wellington Manor residents had been assured by ACML that everything would remain the same for the village. However, this is not what happened, and the Residents Association found themselves constantly battling with the new owners to live up to their promise that everything would remain the same for the village.

In mid-November, Martin contacted Ms Smith, the ACML Queensland General Manager, to advise that Roberta was going to move in with him but did not wish to be included on the deeds of the villa. She advised that there were three options (see below) and that ACML would draw up a Long Term Guest Licence allowing Roberta to live in the village but without the rights of a normal resident. In the expectancy of this option becoming a satisfactory solution, Roberta gave notice that she would be vacating her rental home on the Gold Coast on February 11th and that she would take approximately half of her belongings to Martin's and store the rest. Martin sold some of his furniture to make room for her furniture.

During these early discussions and correspondence they were told that there were three options to allow Roberta to move into the village:

1. If Martin wanted Roberta to be part owner of the property, he would have to sell his property, pay the full exit fees, and buy it back at whatever value given by the retirement village operators or

2. Roberta would have to sign the aforementioned 'Long Term Guest Licence' that allowed her to live with Martin. They would have to pay $700 for this licence. [There is no mention of such a licence in the Queensland Retirement Villages Act of 1999.] This was accompanied by an 11-page car parking licence and that Roberta would pay $50 per month for parking in an open space visitors car park or,

3. Roberta could stay for three weeks, leave the village for one day and repeat the process.

None of these options were fully acceptable to them. The first option was met with open-mouthed amazement that the owners could have the gall to suggest it. Where else in Australia do you have to sell your home and then buy it back in order to have a partner move in with you? The letter from Ms. Smith [January 14, 2008)] to Mr. Williams stated:

'As previously advised, should Ms Cava wish to be considered a resident for the purposes of the Act, then the existing residence contract that you have entered into would need to be terminated and a new residence contract (in your name and Ms Cava's name) would need to be entered into. Of course, this will trigger payment of any exit fees under your current residence contract, the issue of a new Public Information document to both parties and the payment of a new ingoing contribution.'

This new PID (Public Information Document) would have a maximum exit fee of 36% - not the 30% fee that is in Martin's existing PID. They decided that this option was out of the question, not only because it appeared unfair, but because it also appeared to be a case of 'double-dipping' of exit fees. Besides, Martin couldn't afford to lose 50% of his equity in his home.

Martin pointed out to Ms. Smith that under the previous Scheme with operators/owners, other residents in the village had re-married. The Manor Group had directed their lawyers to add the new partner as a village resident paying just the normal legal fees to change the document without adding (in some cases) their partner to the PID. They did not have to sell and re-buy their own properties as he was told he had to do. This made no difference to ACML's decision.

The 'Long Term Guest Licence.' was delivered in mid-December, and ACML encouraged them to take the three-page document to a lawyer. They did so, but couldn't get an appointment until the second week in January. Their lawyer asked them who had prepared the document. There were so many errors and omissions in it that he suggested that it had been thrown together by a legal clerk – certainly not by a qualified lawyer. Their lawyer advised that any agreement signed by the resident, guest and owners was in fact a contract, and not a licence, to allow relatives, carer's etc., to move into the retirement village and be free to use the village facilities. He advised us to remove two clauses because they absolved the Operators of their 'Duty of Care' responsibilities:

1. 'Releases the Operator from all liability (whether in contract, tort, by statute or otherwise however) in respect of all claims whatever relating to, the use and occupation of the Unit by the Guest and the residing within the Village by the Guest.'

2. 'The Guest releases and indemnifies the Operator and agrees to keep the Operator and its employees, agents and contractors released and at all times indemnified to the fullest extent permitted by law from and against all claims of every description whatever incurred by the Operator or for which the Operator may be or become liable whether in contract, tort, by statute or otherwise however and during or after the term of the Licence in respect of or arising from, the use and occupation of the Unit by the Guest and the residing in the Village by the Guest.'

They also objected to the clause that stated:

3. 'If the Resident dies or vacates the Unit ('in this clause, collectively referred to as the Resident Leave Date') and the Guest has prior to the Resident Leave Date occupied the Unit pursuant to this Licence for less than six (6) months, and the Guest is occupying the Unit at the Resident Leave Date - by the Operator giving the Guest at least thirty (30) days written notice that this Licence is terminated and the Guest is required to vacate the Unit.'

They felt this clause was very cruel and would be very traumatic for Roberta (or anyone else in that position) to be forced out of a unit thirty days after a partner had died. The lawyer also advised that there was nothing in the contract protecting Martin, should their relationship break up, so he added a new item,

'The licence expires on the termination of the relationship of the guest and the resident.'

He also advised that because the licence was a template for many similar situations, there should be no charge to the resident. He also questioned the legal fee of $700 for a standard legal document that likely took about fifteen minutes to prepare (meaning the 'lawyer' would be earning approximately $2,800 per hour). In fact, because the document had to be re-written, he advised us that we should not be paying any legal fee charged by the ACML.

The third option (stay three weeks – out one day, etc.) seemed rather an absurd suggestion. It certainly would not be a viable option.

On Friday, January 18th, just one day before Martin and Roberta were to take a planned two-week vacation to New Zealand, they took the revised Long Term Guest Licence to a Justice of the Peace and had it witnessed. They also signed a cohabitation agreement and had it witnessed.

That same day a meeting was held with Ms Michelle Smith and Diane Brown of ACML. From the commencement of this meeting, Ms Smith systematically criticised and refused to accept virtually every amendment made by their solicitor to the Long Term Guest Licence. She further humiliated them by implying that they had wasted their money and that if Roberta wished to live in the village it would be on her (ACML's) terms with no give or take. Roberta naturally took exception to this dictatorial attitude and resented being treated in such a derogatory manner.

A heated discussion ensued, especially in relation to the charges for the 'licence' and the alternative of selling the villa with all its exit fees. Roberta stated that, in her view, ACML was taking advantage of elderly people who were captive to the terms of the retirement village operators. Ms Smith took exception to this and stated that she was considering withdrawing the 'offer' of the Long Term Guest Licence. Because of this implied threat to discriminate against her and for the loss of her civil liberty, Roberta gathered the documents together and stormed out of the meeting. Before Martin left the meeting, he stated that he would get the document to their lawyer and have it re-instated to meet ACML rules, but because they were leaving on holiday the next day (Saturday) they could not have the document signed again by a Justice of the Peace until they returned on February 4th. Ms Smith subsequently denied that Martin had made this comment!

When Roberta checked her mail upon her return from NZ, she saw that the lawyer had adapted the document to suit ACML. Martin also received a letter from Ms. Smith in which it stated that ACML were formally withdrawing their offer of a Long Term Guest Licence due to Roberta's 'attitude to retirement living.' Ms Smith also stated that Roberta had to report to ACML every time she stayed overnight in the unit:

'We confirm that any future visits to the Village by Ms Cava will be governed by the terms of your lease and in particular, please ensure that the notice requirements under clause 11.18 for intended overnight stays are adhered to.'

She also objected to Roberta's use of profanity (She used the words 'that stinks' and 'crap' to describe her opinion of option number one - a view taken by virtually everyone in the village they spoke to later).

ACML dumped this disastrous news on them one week before the removalists were coming to collect Roberta's belongings. They just sat there looking at each other thinking, *'What are we going to do?'* Martin decided he would attempt to get Ms Smith to reconsider the contents of her letter. He left two telephone calls for her, which she finally answered at noon on Wednesday and stated that even if he were to marry Roberta, she would not be allowed to move into his home.

With five days left till Roberta's planned move, she began frantically searching for a new home close to where Martin lived. Luckily, on Thursday she found a unit that she was able to move into four days later on February 11th. Because they cannot share expenses as planned, this adds over $1,500 per month to Roberta's expenses.

Shortly after becoming settled in her new home in Capalaba, Roberta noticed that $88,000 of her superannuation investments were with AMP. She promptly pulled out of those investments and sent a letter to Craig Dunn CEO of AMP explaining why she had removed the funds. She subsequently received an answer to that letter from Glen Brown, the CEO of ACML in which he stated:

'I have fully reviewed the results of these investigations and confirm that all ACML staff involved have acted appropriately and that our decision to withdraw the previous offer stands.'

At no time did Glen Brown interview either Martin or Roberta.

Because Queensland does not have its own Human Rights Act, laws to protect civil and individual rights, it is difficult for them to fight back in this situation. They are absolutely appalled that ACML has the law on their side and are allowed to discriminate as they have. They are currently taking advice from the legal department of the Association of Residents of Queensland Retirement Villages Inc. (ARQRV).

It is worth noting that on April 15th an article appeared in the Australian Financial Post stating that AMP Capital Investors and Meridien Group were splitting and that the entire portfolio could come to the market in coming months. So possibly Meridien Lifestyle will be forced to sell Wellington Manor and Roberta and Martin could then try again with a new scheme operator that uses more compassion and common sense when dealing with seniors. If the village is not sold, Roberta and Martin will have to expend further money in legal fees trying to fight for their right to live together against the huge legal resources of ACML. What chance do they have and what a dreadful way to treat seniors in the twilight years of their lives.

Martin and Roberta's hopes and recommendations are:

1. That the Queensland Retirement Village Act be entirely re-written so that the rights of the Residents are equally represented with those given to Operators. The Act does not cover:

   a) What would happen if a resident dies, and the other person decides to re-marry or live with a partner in their unit.

   b) What should happen if a partner wants to move in without putting his/her name on the PID of the unit.

   c) Whether 'Long Term Guest Licences' are legal.

2. That potential residents proposing to move into a Retirement Village property are completely aware of how much money the Operators are really taking from them should they die or decide to sell their units.

3. That Queensland residents ensure that a Human Rights Act or Bill of Rights (similar to that in the ACT and other states) is ratified, so that Queensland residents can fight situations such as ours.

[In addition: I sent the following information relating to discrimination:]

Martin and I feel that Meridien have violated the following acts:

1. Insisting that I sign a Long Term Guest Licence. There is no mention of such an agreement in the Retirement Village Act.

2. The Queensland Anti Discrimination Act, 1991 states:

Discrimination of certain types prohibited:

    8. The Act prohibits the following types of discrimination ...

9.   (a) direct discrimination;

    (b) indirect discrimination

Meaning of direct discrimination

10. (1) Direct discrimination of the basis of an attribute happens if a person treats, or proposes to treat, a person with an attribute less favourably than another person without the attribute is or would be treated in circumstances that are the same or not materially different.

(2) It is not necessary that the person who discriminates considers the treatment is less favourable.

(3) The person's motive for discriminating is irrelevant.

(4) If there are 2 or more reasons why a person treats, or proposes to treat, another person with an attribute less favourably, the person treats the other person less favourably on the basis of the attribute if the attribute is a substantial reason for the treatment.

Division 8 – Accommodation area

Subdivision A – Prohibitions in accommodation area

Explanatory provision (prohibitions)

81. A person must not discriminate in the accommodation area if a prohibition in section 82 to 85 applies.

Discrimination in pre-accommodation area

82. A person must not discriminate against another person –

    (a) By failing to accept an application for accommodation; or

    (b) By failing to renew or extend the supply of accommodation; or

    (c) In the way in which an application is processed; or

    (d) In the terms on which accommodation is offered, renewed or extended.

Discrimination in accommodation area

83. A person must not discriminate against another person –

   (a) In any variation of the terms on which accommodation is supplied; or
   (b) In denying or limiting access to any benefit associated with the accommodation; or
   (c) In evicting the other person from the accommodation; or
   (d) By treating the other person unfavourably in any way in connection with the accommodation.

29 April, 5:00 pm

Hi Martin,

Here's the correspondence I have had with Karryn Cooper of Today Tonight (Channel 7). She called after she sent this message and I gave her a bit of information, and she was as they say in Australia 'gobsmacked' at the information and wanted to do an interview right away. I told her we were going to the Gold Coast tomorrow afternoon, so she asked if she could come at 9:30 tomorrow. I told her that would be fine with me, but I needed to check it out with you.

Talk to you later tonight. Love, R.

29 April, 5:00 pm

(Our emails overlapped, so I was not aware of the following:)

Hi Roberta

I want to speak to ARQRV legal of what I am intending to do. I also need to know categorically that Meridien cannot obtain an eviction order for breaching my lease. My PID, Deed of Occupation (lease) and the Act are very vague on this aspect.

Love M

29 April, 5:06 pm

Hello Karryn

I've spoken with Martin Williams and he says 9:30 am tomorrow morning would be fine. His address is (gave address) that is on the right side almost opposite side of the street to the Leisure Centre). His phone number is (gave number).

Best regards,

Roberta Cava

29 April, 10:24 pm

(I was surprised to receive the following email from Martin, especially since we had been discussing this issue for days and had worked so diligently to prepare the media release.)

Hi Roberta,

You (we) have always said that we should be honest in our dealings with each other, so I will be quite open about my present concerns.

Firstly, why did you go ahead with the TV interview and not respect my wishes in the email I sent earlier today? I find it rather disappointing and quite stressful that you have overridden my wishes without further discussion on the matter.

Originally you said that you would give ARQRV time to arrive at a solution and that if it was unsatisfactory, you, because of your media experience, would go to the media. I agree that after eight weeks of minimal activity you should go ahead. However, more recently you have indicated that I, rather than you, should approach the media, despite my concerns about the lease and my position as a 'visitor' awaiting residency, plus lack of media experience. Now you have gone ahead and arranged an interview involving both of us at my villa tomorrow rather than on neutral ground. The arrival of a car with a Channel 7 News logo at my villa will circulate through the village like wildfire and spark off all sorts of rumours.

As you well know, the producer will edit the interview for maximum impact and show excerpts from our statements rather than the full sentence and not be interested in our aims, or concerns. Therefore, as I said on the phone earlier tonight, it is important that nothing is said that cannot be physically supported by written proof and I rely upon your help and guidance in this matter and hope that we can devise and agree the strategy prior to their arrival.

I have to admit that I am not comfortable with the sudden turn of events but am sure that I will rise to the occasion when the camera starts turning providing we fully support each other.

I will try not to have bags under my eyes but doubt I will sleep well!!

Love, Martin

I phoned him and told him that if he was reluctant to do the interview I would do it myself. He said he would think it over and let me know in the morning.

I did not sleep at all that night as I went over what I would say that would not get me in trouble the next day during the interview. I looked very haggard in the morning and knew that the television people would be coming about 9:30 am to do the interview.

30 April, (Wednesday) 6:21 am

I too didn't sleep much last night mulling over what I could and could not say.

I'm sorry you feel that I have not dealt with your reluctance to go to the media. I was patient for over eight weeks for ARQRV to do something about our situation, but it appears that they are not going to do anything.

As to your fear that you will be thrown out of the village – they would have no grounds upon which to do so, and as far as keeping you from staying in Australia – what has that got to do with us simply defending ourselves against a company? We have given Meridien every opportunity to change their decision, have found out that we can't depend on the laws of Australia to do it for us, so this was the only option left to us. In fact we have discussed this option several times. I felt the timing was right especially with the pending split between AMP and Meridien.

You did approve of us going to the Courier Mail and have mentioned that Channel 9 is interested in new stories – so don't understand how is this different' You have enough experience with a microphone to deal with a TV interview – far better than most, so can't understand your fear about the interview. I realise that if we hadn't made the move right now, it might never be taken because you seemed to be dragging your feet about it. I felt that it was now or never, and seeing it involved you and Wellington Manor directly, felt that was the place where the interview should be held.

I will call the TV lady and say that you don't want to do the interview and possibly they can just interview me here at my home.

Let me know if you wish to back out and I will do as you wish.

Love, R.

30 April, 6:46 am

Good morning Roberta,

I did not sleep too well either. However, I do feel more comfortable doing an interview away from nosey neighbours and will come over to you at 9.00 or half an hour before whatever time Channel 7 agree to.

I will attempt to speak to someone in ARQRV before coming over to let them know what we are doing.

See you soon

Love M

30 April, 7:30 am

Hi Martin

I've just left a message with the TV lady that changes the venue for the interview by asking her to have it here at my home. You can then decide whether you want to take part in the interview or not.

I've asked her to telephone me to confirm the change. R.

30 April, 9:00 am

[Gavin Alder came with a cameraman. They arrived at 9:00 am and the interview didn't end until almost 4:00 pm. He interviewed us at my townhouse, showed that I was the author of the book Dealing with Difficult People, then we all drove to Martin's villa, where they took shots around Martin's villa and the village recreational centre. At the end, we were filmed taking a stroll along the waterfront at Wellington Point.] They mentioned that they would be doing other interviews about the topic and would let us know when it would be aired.]

Martin was calm, cool and collected during the interview and did most of the talking throughout the interview. We're wondering what they will use on their program and whether they will represent us well. We have no idea when they will air the piece, but hope it will be sooner rather than later so we can take some steps to stop this travesty.

CHAPTER 11
MAY, 2008

2 May, (Friday) 8:36 am

Morning Martin,

When you talked with Gavin did he say he would make a copy of the piece for us? Hopefully it will be a digital one on a CD that we can copy and send to our friends.

Wonder if it will air tonight? If it does, that would be during or just after the Happy Hour? What would you do about that? Would you tell everyone that it will be on?

Love, R

2 May, (Friday) 9:11 am

Hi Roberta,

No we didn't discuss making copies ... the conversation was more about the widening spread of the investigation and checking out some of Meridien's 'false' statements. I am not expecting it to be aired tonight but will probably have a better idea later today. I think Gavin will inform one of us if it is to be tonight. I hope to speak to Les soon to see what happened there yesterday!

Happy Hour starts at 4.30 and I have to go down to set up at 4.00, so if you arrive here after that, let yourself in and come down when you are ready. The outback films start at around 6.30.

See you later, Love M

2 May, (Friday) - Went to Martin's to enjoy the happy hour and movie.

3 May, (Saturday) 9:08 am

Do you have any extra time today? One of the drawers in my big clothes cupboard in my bedroom is giving me grief. The front of the drawer came off and I can't open it. I will need some wood glue and seem to remember that you got some a couple of weeks ago. I might have some dried up stuff myself.

Please let me know. Love, R.

3 May, (Saturday)

Hi Roberta,

I can come over later this morning probably around eleven, then must do some shopping and write two reports for the committee meeting as we are away next week, also have to prepare the May film flyer, so can't stop for long. Do I need to bring any tools to force the drawer open?

Love, M.

4 May (Sunday) – Went to Martin's that evening. As usual had to report to 'mother' that I was staying with him overnight.

5 & 6 May, (Monday and Tuesday) – Took a bus to Stanthorpe with other residents. Stayed at the Stanthorpe Motel. Visited wineries, fruit farms, lavender farms, granite belt and had Italian dinner.

7 May, (Wednesday) – Back to Martin's from Stanthorpe. We were able to watch the Today Tonight show and learn that our piece was going to be featured the next night.

7 May, (Wednesday) - Martin sent the following message to residents:

Dear fellow email residents,

You are probably aware that I lost my wife, Anita, after 44-years of marriage in 2004. As many of you will know, I met Roberta Cava in Feb 2007 and after some eleven months of dating was refused permission by Meridiem Lifestyles for her move into Wellington Manor during February this year as my de-facto partner because neither she, nor I, would sign an illegal document (Long Term Guest Licence) which gave her no residential rights, or liability protection in the event of an accident, plus many other restrictions. The unacceptable alternative was for me to sell my villa, pay the 30% exit fee and then buy back my villa at the current new valuation and increased (Meridien imposed) exit fee of 36%. A cost of $215,000 exit fee, plus a further $200,000 + dollars in the re-purchase of my own villa, in order to add Roberta to my PID ... a factor that neither of us wanted. A total of $400,000 +. Where else in the world does this happen? In a meeting with Michelle Smith, Meridien General

Manager Queensland, to discuss this, Roberta told her that the deal was mercenary, unethical, stank and was 'crap' ... Hence the ban on Roberta for use of profanity!!!

I understand from Gwen & John that the interview of Roberta and myself by a Channel seven investigative reporter, re Meridien Lifestyle imposing the above unsubstantiated restrictions (not supported by the Queensland Retirement Village Act 1999) upon my bringing a partner into my home, is to be shown on the Today Tonight programme between 6.30 and 7.00 pm tomorrow night, Thurs 8th, under the title of a $200,000 ransom!! In fact I think it should read $400,000?? (I just hope that none of you find yourself in this position and support the stand that Roberta and I are taking in exposing this manipulation of the Act in favour of the Scheme operator/owner)

Both Les Armstrong, President of ARQRV (Association of Residents of Queensland Retirement Villages) and village resident Bill Bittel (who also lost his wife, two weeks before I lost Anita) and subsequently brought a new partner into the village without having to sell and re-purchase his villa, are included in the interview with, I understand, comments by Meridien Lifestyles and the State Attorney's Office.

I am reasonably confident that the Channel Seven presentation will be factual and focus upon the injustice without too much sensationalism ... fingers crossed!! Village residents please tell your neighbours to switch on to channel seven Today Tonight ... also, before passing judgment, consider what action you would take if you were in this position during your twilight years?

The fact that I am currently President of Wellington Manor Residents Association Inc. is irrelevant to the above scenario and I trust that you will keep both aspects completely separate.

Regards, Martin Williams

May 7, (Wednesday) 8:18 am

Hi Martin,

When you come over this afternoon could you please bring two things:

1. The boxes of books I still have stored in your storage room. There are about 16 books in each box and Delphine is likely going to order about 50 of them - so I will need them handy to send to her.

2. A copy of the Today Tonight DVD.

Thanks, R.

8 May, (Thursday) – Our story was aired on Today Tonight entitled '200,000 Ransom!'

Anna Coren was the TV announcer who covered our piece. She opened the program by introducing us and explaining the problems we were facing. Martin stated, *'Where else in Australia do you have to sell your home and then buy it back in order to take in a partner.'*

Martin talked about how he and his wife Anita had emigrated from England and had moved into the retirement village. His wife died of breast cancer and two years later he met me and we started dating. It showed pictures of Martin's lovely home and other parts of the village. Martin stated that other couples in the village had lost partners and they were able to move into the village, so didn't think our situation would be a problem. The problem was it wasn't our decision to make – it was Meridien's. Darren explained that we had negotiated with Michelle Smith and explained the three options she gave us.

Later that week Gavin interviewed Bill Bittel and his partner Brenda who had been accepted into the village by the previous owners (Manor Group) without the problems we faced for a fee of $3,000. They identified Meridien as being a very large conglomerate owning $1 billion dollars worth of Retirement Villages (25 of them) as well as in excess of $4 billion in other developments throughout Queensland. Gavin mentioned that Meridien had been featured in newspaper articles stating what a gold mine aged care was, but did not discuss what they charge residents. Gavin also interviewed Les Armstrong, the President of ARQRV (Association of Residents of Queensland Retirement Villages) who enlightened them more on our problem. He stated that what Meridien had done was above board according to the Queensland Retirement Village Act, but was it morally right?

Martin ended our section of the program by stating, *'I am not allowed to live with the woman I love. I cannot make a free choice to bring that person into my villa and I find that sad and upsetting and morally wrong.'*

Lastly - they did not show Michelle Smith, but stated that Meridien had said, *'Mr. Williams never asked for a Joint Tenancy Agreement. If he had the most it would have cost would have been $1,000.'*

[Readers, again note what Michelle Smith said about a Joint Tenancy Agreement in her email of January 14, 2008:

'As previously advised, should Ms Cava wish to be considered a resident for the purposes of the Act, then the existing residence contract that you have entered into would need to be terminated and a new residence contract (in your name and Ms Cava's name) would need to be entered into. Of course, this will trigger payment of any exit fees under your current residence contract, the issue of a new Public Information Document to both parties and the payment of a new ingoing contribution.'

Under those terms it would not have cost Martin $1,000, but $215,000+.]

We were very disappointed about the final comments on the program which allowed Meridien to lie about our options. [Channel 7 **did** have the information in writing about the options given by Ms Smith, but they did not mention this to refute Meridien's comments.]

9 May, (Friday) - I attended a Probus meeting.

9 May, (Friday) 2:03 pm

Hi Les,

Thanks for speaking on our behalf for the Today Tonight segment.

I haven't received a reply to the email I sent to you on April 9th about the book I want to write. Could you please let me know whether you are still willing to help me write that book and provide me with the information I need to do so?

Also, Martin mentioned that Today Tonight might interview you about ARQRV exclusively. Do you know when they might be doing that?

One thing I need confirmation of: Is a Long Term Guest Licence mentioned in the Retirement Village Act? I couldn't find it anywhere, so wonder if it is indeed a legal document they wanted us to sign. I also wonder if they pulled their offer of having me sign one because it *was* illegal?

I hope to hear from you soon.

Best regards,

Roberta Cava

9 May, (Friday) 7:49 am to Karryn Cooper Today Tonight

Subject: $200,000 ransom

Hello Karryn,

Thank you for doing our piece called '$200,000 Ransom' last night.

I know it's hard to get everything onto a five-minute segment, but I was disappointed that you gave AMP Meridien the last word in the segment where they said that I could be put on the PID for just $1,000. This comment was not correct as was proven by the information that was enclosed in an email sent by Michelle Smith of Meridien to Martin Williams on January 14th that stated,

'As previously advised, should Ms Cava wish to be considered a resident for the purposes of the Act, then the existing residence contract that you have entered into would need to be terminated and a new residence contract (in your name and Ms Cava's name) would need to be entered into. Of course, this will trigger payment of any exit fees under your current residence contract, the issue of a new Public Information Document to both parties and payment of a new ingoing contribution.'

Gavin had filmed this comment in the email, but it was not shown to refute AMP Meridien's statement.

Also not mentioned was that the Long Term Guest Licence provided by Meridien that we were expected to sign is not mentioned in the Retirement Village Act, so therefore to my knowledge would not have been a legal document under that Act.

The reason we contacted the media was because we wanted two things to happen:

1. That the Queensland Government would change the Retirement Village Act so that it not only protected the operators of the villages, but the residents as well.
2. To warn anyone who was interested in going into a Retirement Village to be very careful before they signed on the dotted line and to ask lots of questions about their rights such as:
   a. What if I don't like living in the village?
   b. What will I have to pay to move out in say 6 months if I don't like my neighbours?
   c. What if I become ill and need a carer to live with me?
   d. What if my spouse dies and I want to have a relative, new spouse or partner move in with me?

I have my doubts whether anything will change for Martin and me, because all those important details were left out of the segment.

Best regards,

Roberta Cava

[I did not receive a reply to this email.]

9 May, (Friday)

Martin received a cautionary letter from one of his friends in the village to warn him not to bring up the television program at the village Happy Hour that evening. This was because many residents had been swayed to believe Meridien's side of the story because at that morning's tea, he was led to believe, that Michelle was still repeating untruths regarding the situation to the residents.

He added that both Martin and I had nothing but support, but others could ruin the Happy Hour evening.

So we listened and did not discuss the issue but I felt even more animosity towards Michelle at her continuing devious actions.

10 May, (Saturday)

Hi Martin

I've just re-read the Retirement Village Act and was surprised that it was written in such a way that the resident was protected. The only thing missing was that it didn't cover situations such as ours or the need to have a carer, relative, new spouse or partner joins the resident in the unit. However, I did note some sections of the Act that seem to protect us such as:

*25 Urgent Applications. (Tribunals) Ours was certainly urgent at the time.

Urgent applications can be made to the Tribunal in circumstances:

- where a resident is threatened with removal from the village; [They almost forced you to leave by saying I couldn't join you.]
- where use of the village is restricted; or
- when threatened with deprivation e.g. being transferred to a unit of a lesser standard. [I was not allowed to move in with you.]
- There are many reasons why you might want to move. They include changing health, family and financial circumstances. The new Act has a better process for the resale of a resident's unit. Resale means selling your 'right to reside' in the village. Important wording! (right to reside). [You don't want to sell your unit because you want to reside in the village with me.]
- The resident and the scheme operator must agree in writing on the resale value of the accommodation unit within 30 days of the date that the resident's right to reside in the village is terminated. [You do not want to terminate your right to reside in the village!]
- Fees/charges and entitlements when leaving.
- There are fees, accrued charges and a final exit entitlement which you must consider when leaving the village.

Specific points to remember:

- There is an exit fee to which the operator is entitled as specified in your contract and PID. It is payable when you leave or upon settlement and is usually deducted before you receive your exit entitlement. [You're not leaving!]

Just food for thought ... R.

May 10, (Saturday)

Last night almost as soon as I walked in the door at Martin's he snapped at me. He was in the process of writing a letter to Michelle Smith and wanted me to look at it. I said, *'I hope you are challenging her about the offer she made on TV that my name could be put on the title for $1,000.'* he snapped *'Just come and look at what I've written before you tell me what to do.'* That started the evening and I almost went home at that point.

He showed me the film clip of our TV appearance and realised how much they had crammed into five minutes of film. We then went to the leisure centre for a going-away Master Chef dinner for John and Gwen.

I was very quiet all night and could hardly eat a thing. I was shunned by some residents. There was a lot of banter at the table and some used the word 'crap' in their conversation just to be funny and show support to me. I laughed but didn't talk about the program. All in all, it was a pleasant evening.

When we got back to Martin's he brought up the issue with Michelle again and I said that he would have to negotiate with her – that I could not even be civil to her. We ended up in a heated argument and he stated that he was tempted to move back to England; but he could not do so because of the cats. I asked him *'And what about me?'* I'd had quite a bit of wine and almost shouted it at him.

He didn't reply. He left my bedroom and shortly after he left the room, I got dressed, packed my overnight bag with all my stuff from the bedroom and bathroom and left. [I only had about 10 blocks to drive – but I should not have been driving.]

11 May, (Sunday) - I decided to go away for a few days knowing that I didn't have anything until Friday when I had arranged to go on a bus trip with the ladies' Probus Group. I needed to get away from the mess for a bit and think things through as to what was the best solution to the stress and tension we were under. I contacted my friend Elaine Hollingsworth, the owner of the Hippocrates Health Centre and retreat on the Gold Coast. She offered me one of her rooms and I gratefully accepted it.

I drove to the Gold Coast feeling very sad and isolated. It was Mother's Day and my children and grandchildren were all in Canada, so knew I would not hear from them while I was away.

12 May, (Monday) – I drove to Tamborine Mountain and visited my friend Doreen for lunch, did a bit of shopping for quick food then went back to the retreat.

12 May (Letter sent by Meridien to residents of Wellington Manor. The underscores are hers.)

12 May, 2008 *26

The Residents Retirement Village

269 Birkdale Road
Birkdale Qld 4159

Dear Residents,

We would like to take this opportunity to extend our sincere thanks and appreciation for the overwhelming support that we have received from residents prior to and following the recent airing of a story on the Today Tonight programme. We have been inundated with emails, letters, telephone calls and residents speaking with us. We also wish to take this opportunity to provide an overview on the manner in which a resident is able to have a companion permanently reside with him or her in their villa.

The resident has recently stated that, in order for a companion to permanently reside with them, they had to first terminate their existing residence contract, sell their villa, pay fees under the residence contract (e.g. Exit Fee and capital gain) and then re-purchase the villa at market value.

We wish to advise residents that this is not the case and that this has never been the policy of AMP Capital Meridien Lifestyle.

Should a resident desire to have a companion reside with them, there are broadly two options available to residents.

The options are:

1. By mutual agreement, the existing residents' residence contract is terminated and a new residence contract (including Lease and Public Information Document) is entered into with the existing resident and their companion (**'Joint Tenancy Arrangement'**); or

2. The companion is granted a licence permitting him or her to reside with the existing resident as a permanent guest **(Long Term Guest Licence')**

The implications of either a Joint Tenancy Agreement or a Long Term Guest Licence differ in important ways. Below is an overview of how each arrangement works.

Joint Tenancy Arrangement

From a legal perspective, when the existing residence contract is terminated, payment of certain fees (e.g. Exit Fee, capital gain etc.) would be triggered. A new ongoing contribution would also be payable under the new residence contract.

However, pursuant to AMP Capital Meridien Lifestyle's policy, these fees are not actually paid by the existing resident. These fees are simply transferred over to the new residence contract and the terms and conditions of the existing residence contract remain in force – i.e. the existing resident is, effectively, in the same position as if the existing residence contract was still on foot. The only difference is that the companion becomes a joint resident under the residence contract and a joint tenant under the lease.

As the companion would be considered a 'joint tenant' under Queensland property laws, the companion would be entitled to receive the full exit entitlement upon the resale of the villa (despite what may be prescribed in your Will), if you pre-deceased your companion. Because of this, some residents do not choose this option. Instead, they elect to enter into a Long Term Guest Licence.

Long Term Guest Licence

Long Term Guest Licences are a legitimate means by which an existing resident is able to have a companion permanently reside with them. **They are not illegal documents** as has been suggested by a resident and are permitted by Queensland property laws.

Under this agreement, the companion is not considered a 'resident' for the purposes of the *Retirement Villages Act 1999* **('Act')** and accordingly, would not share with the existing resident any financial obligations or benefits under the residence contract. However, the companion would be able to have the same use and enjoyment of communal facilities within the village as a resident.

In the event that the existing resident pre-deceased their companion, or permanently vacated the Village, the Act permits the companion to continue to reside in the villa for a period of three (3) months, during which time the companion may be asked to enter into a residence contract at the village. Long Term Guest Licences we have recently offered to residents have complied with the section of the Act. They have also afforded proposed guests more rights than prescribed under the Act.

Our advice to residents who may be considering having a companion permanently reside with them is to liaise directly with us. Should you choose to have a companion reside with you, we will also strongly encourage you to seek independent legal and/or financial advice from a professional who is familiar with the Act and Queensland property laws and to also discuss your decision with your family.

If you do have any queries, please do not hesitate to contact us.

Once again, we sincerely thank residents for their overwhelming support.

Yours faithfully,

Wellington Manor Pty Ltd
Michelle Smith
General Manager, Queensland

[I'd like to again bring the reader's attention to the information that was sent to Martin Williams by Michelle Smith regarding a Joint Tenancy Agreement. At no time did she explain the terms as outlined in the above letter. Instead, she had sent the following:]

'As previously advised, should Ms Cava wish to be considered a resident for the purposes of the Act, then the existing residence contract that you have entered into would need to be terminated and a new residence contract (in your name and Ms Cava's name) would need to be entered into. Of course, this will trigger payment of any exit fees under your current residence contract, the issue of a new Public Information Document to both parties and the payment of a new ingoing contribution.'

[Regarding her assertion that the Long Term Guest Licence did not include illegal clauses, I bring the reader's attention to the following clauses:]

3. **OCCUPATION OF UNIT**

(ii) Releases the Operator from all Liability (whether in contract, tort, by statute or otherwise however) in respect of all claims whatever relating to, the use and occupation of the Unit by the Guest and the residing within the Village by the Guest.

5. **GUEST TO INDEMNIFY OPERATOR**

The Guest releases and indemnifies the Operator and agrees to keep the Operator and its employees, agents and contractors released and at all times indemnified to the fullest extent permitted by law from and against all claims of every description whatever incurred by the Operator or for which the Operator may be or become liable whether in contract, tort, by statute or otherwise however and whether during or after the term of the Licence in respect of or arising from, the use and occupation of the Unit by the Guest and the residing in the Village by the Guest.

[Legally Meridien have a duty of care to protect <u>anyone</u> coming into the retirement village from being injured while on their common property – whether they are residents, workers, or guests.]

[They quoted the following clause in the Long Term Agreement:]

'In the event that the existing resident pre-deceased their companion, or permanently vacated the Village, the Act permits the companion to continue to reside in the villa for a period of three (3) months, during which time the companion may ask to enter into a residence contract at the village.'

Our agreement stated:

4. *(iii) If the resident dies or vacates the Unit ('in this clause, collectively referred to as the 'Resident Leave Date'), and the Guest has prior to the Resident Leave Date occupied the Unit pursuant to this Licence for less than six (6) months, and the Guest is occupying the Unit at the Resident Leave Date – by the Operator giving the Guest at least **thirty (30) days** written notice that this Licence is terminated and the Guest is required to vacate the Unit.*

May 13, (Tuesday) – While still staying at the retreat, I visited Babette for coffee then went back to the retreat.

13 May, (Tuesday)

Hi Roberta,

I am still at a loss, and very disappointed, as to why you walked out on Saturday night, especially as you would have been over the limit for driving.

I would not have thought that having a disagreement was the reason as we have had those before, so can only presume that the aggravation and stress of the last few weeks had got to you.

As you have not returned my call, or contacted me, I can only presume that you either want time on your own and will not be attending the ex-services lunch at the Sporting Club tomorrow, or you wish to terminate our relationship, which will be a shame without further discussion/

Please let me know your intentions.

Martin

14 May, (Wednesday) – I drove back to Capalaba.

That evening I phoned Martin and asked him if he could come over the next day. While at the retreat I had decided that we were in a lose/lose situation. He couldn't leave the Village and I was not welcome there except by his close friends. I did not know anyone in the Capalaba area except his friends in the village and because I felt so alienated when I attended any of their functions, I couldn't see how our relationship could continue. I still had three months left on my lease and that would mean that I had to stay in the area until it ran out, or I would find another place and pay double rent. It would depend on what Martin had to say when I spoke with him.

15 May

Martin came over and we talked. I explained how alienated I felt when I came into the village – how Michelle had turned the residents against me and even if I was able to move in with him – things would always be strained. He kept saying, *'I'm sorry for what I've put you through.'*

He said we could continue as we were – each of us staying in our own homes. I explained that I didn't want to stay in his unit overnight any more, that I strongly objected to having to report to 'mother' every time I stayed there. He asked me if I would still go to functions in the village and to take me out to dinner. He said he wanted to remain friends and I said that I did as well. So we will just see each other socially.

After Martin left, I felt as if a huge weight had been taken off my shoulders. The only strong emotion I still felt was terrible anger at Michelle Smith for her vindictive actions. I still intended to fight her for her slanderous actions, but would try to leave Martin out of the equation.

16 May, (Friday) – I went on a bus trip with our ladies Probus Club. One of the club members (Delma McLaughlin who is a resident of the village) snubbed me as we waited for the bus to pick us up just outside the retirement village. She looked at me and intentionally turned her back to me. This ruined the bus trip for me and just added fuel to the rejection I felt.

18 May, (Sunday)

Sunday – I had Frank, Amelia and Martin for lasagne dinner at my townhouse. It was a nice evening and I felt good being with this couple.

19 May, (Monday)

Hi Roberta,

Many thanks for the dinner last night. It was a nice relaxed evening with friends and I know that Frank and Amelia both enjoyed it. They think your house and location is very good.

We bottled 72 bottles of wine this morning without making too much mess!! It just remains to get the labels printed and we are in business.

Your link to the TV program works very well so I have sent it to family and friends in England. Presumably it takes the full 20 minutes to download in dial-up so I hope most of them have broadband.

Thanks again for last night.

Martin

23 May, (Friday) 5:38 pm

Subject: Wynnam News

Hi Martin,

I just got a call from the Wynnum News. The chief editor will be doing an article about us for next week's paper. They can't believe our story is true and are really disgusted at Meridien's actions.

Hope you approve.

Cheers, R.

23 May, 7:17 pm

Subject: Wynnam News

Hi Roberta,

Good if they pick up on the omissions and incorrect statement at the end of the program. The distribution of Wynnum News is naturally very small and will not be seen in the village so is unlikely to embarrass Meridien but it should give the opportunity to put the record straight.

How do they intend to interview?

Cheers, Martin

23 May, 9:16 pm

Hi Roberta,

I should have asked this earlier. Given that that you no longer have any wish to continue with our relationship on a romantic level and do not wish to move into the village, what are you hoping to achieve from an interview with Wynnum News?

I will forward an email that shows I have already lost support from members of the village in dealing with Meridien because of the TV program.

It is important for me to know what is behind your thinking.

Cheers, Martin

24 May, (Saturday) 7:41 am

Hi Martin,

I can see that you have talked to Lorna and John again and they have suggested that you ask me the enclosed questions.

The Wynnum News had the information before we went on TV and I sent them an update soon after it was filmed. It simply took them that long to reply. I'm not finished with Meridien - they are not going to get away with doing such things to seniors in the future. Michelle is a serial bully, and I will make sure she has to account for her bullying behaviour. That is a separate issue from ours even though her bullying tactics are what triggered my actions.

By your comment *'I will forward an email that shows I have already lost support from members of the village in dealing with Meridien because of the TV program.'* - because I set it up - I guess that's my fault. Sorry if my defensive actions against this bully are causing you grief.

R.

[He did not send that letter to me.]

24 May, (Saturday) 7:41 am

Morning Roberta,

No, I have not spoken to Lorna for over a week so they have no idea about the Wynnum approach. I just wanted to know what you feel you will achieve going to a local paper - hence my questions.

I think the internal problems with certain members of my committee wishing to kowtow to Meridien and not make waves will continue. At least I know who they are. M

24 May, (Saturday) 7:56 am

Hello Phil, [*Phil Wise – lawyer for Resident's Association*]

I'm hoping you can help me. I'm the person that's taken on Meridien about not allowing me to move into the Wellington Manor with Martin Williams.

I've sent several emails to Les Armstrong, trying to get the information he was going to send me. As you probably know, he has agreed to supply information to me that will assist me in getting together a book I expect to write: *'Dealing with Retirement Village Bullies.'*

However, he has not replied and I wonder if you could supply me with the information instead. I would be willing to come to Buderim to pick up the information if you are unable to put it together for me.

One of the most important things I need is a letter giving me permission to use the information you give to me. Another is details on tribunals that have taken place in the past and the resolutions by the courts and the third is the contact people in other states that might be willing to contribute to the book.

Can you help?

Best regards,

Roberta Cava

28 May, (Wednesday) 8:49 am – [I thought I'd see for myself how the residents responded to having me on the village premises ...]

Hi Martin,

Am I still invited to the Master Chef dinner on Friday?

Cheers, R.

28 May, (Wednesday) 11:10 am

Hi Roberta,

Yes, of course!! You are seated on the Master chef table along with Amelia, Judy Redpath and Joyce Warne ... all the men on the table will of course be working and join you for the meal. Barry and Juanita have some family problems and will not be there.

I was going to contact you today to check if you wanted to stay overnight after the meal as I need to make the bed up? I have been doing some sheets and blankets spring cleaning, throwing out fridge use by dates and sorting out clothes for Angela's Church collection for Aboriginal communities at Cunnamulla. Could you let me know if you will be staying? You will need to be at the hall at around 5.00 pm and you have a key if you want to drop off an overnight bag first. I presume I will have to be cooking shortly after 4.00 pm.

Roger has been back to his usual vet and has not coughed for over a day since, so the pills must be working!!

Looks as if we may be lucky with some rain today.

Cheers, M

28 May, (Wednesday) 4:38 pm

Hi Martin,

I'll be off to see Les Armstrong tomorrow afternoon. He will be putting some things together for me and will help in any way he can. I will tell you all about it when I see you on Friday.

Re: Friday night, I will watch how much I drink - so will be able to drive home okay. No need to make up the room.

Cheers, R.

29 May, (Thursday) – Martin and I drove to Les Armstrong's villa for a meeting and to obtain many pages of information that could help us fight Meridien.

30 May (Friday) - Master Chef dinner. I felt very alienated by the residents and wondered why I was still coming to the Village events. A hopeless situation.

31 May, (Saturday)

Hi Martin,

I'm concerned that you are feeling alienated by the Wellington Manor residents. What has Michelle said to the residents that have made you feel this way? I was surprised to learn that 60% of the residents were against our situation.

Can you give me more details?

I still care about you. Roberta.

May 31, (Saturday) 10:41 pm

Hi Roberta,

I became aware of a groundswell of opinion against us when Brian advised me not to defend our stance, or pass any comment, at the happy hour, about the injustice of the comment at the end of the TV programme ... you had copies of my response to Brian at that time.

The next day, Meridien held a morning tea presentation at which, I understand Michelle, in answer to a question from a resident, very craftily stated that we had misrepresented the true situation and (I have no proof) said that your attitude towards Meridien was not conducive to you becoming a resident of the village. It is difficult to argue against their statement because it is true that you lost your composure and allowed yourself to over-react against Michelle. This is a pity because she had already given way on the first point of our argument to allow three months grace if I was to die in the first six months. Had we continued with reasonable argument I think you would now be a resident in my villa and none of the subsequent upheaval would have happened.

On the Monday following the program, Meridien (Michelle) produced a letter to all residents giving miss-information that we (I) had not taken up an alternative option of a Tenancy Agreement. You had a copy of that letter. This was an exercise of miss-information of very little importance to most residents, but would certainly colour any response. I subsequently wrote a truthful denial of Meridien's stances, but was advised by many of my friends, not to distribute it to all residents as it would be counter-productive and not help our cause. I withheld distribution to all letter boxes and have had verbal support from many residents that they are pleased I did not, as it was unlikely to have achieved anything and far better to let all animosity die down.

Subsequently, from reaction of residents who I thought supported me, I have detected a withdrawal of that support. Why! I am not sure. I understand they may perceive you as a very forthright, strongly opinioned person that they cannot deal with and feel threatened by your presence. Alternatively, they may not wish to become involved. How else can you describe Delma McLaughlin's reaction to ignoring you on the Probus trip? She is not a 'friend' of mine so I don't think her reaction was related to me, but may not have wished to be seen as taking sides?

I have to honestly say that I cannot see a solution to carrying on a losing battle with Meridien. You see this as a weakness in my character, but you should understand that I have to continue living here because I cannot afford to lose $215,000 of my retirement capital plus, as president of the association, I am finding my position increasingly undermined.

I too care for you very much and am devastated by your comments and reasons for ending the relationship.

To end on a more cheerful note, the knitted pullover fits fine and is very warm and comfortable, so thanks very much for your labour of love.

Hope you enjoyed last night and sorry I didn't get much time to talk to you. Love, M.

CHAPTER 12
JUNE, 2008

1 June, (Sunday) 10:17 am

Martin,

I'm sorry I caused you so much difficulty at the village by retaliating against the bullying tactics of Michelle Smith. I will not embarrass you further by visiting the village and will get out of your life completely.

I had hoped we could remain friends but it appears that I'm too much of a disruption to your status and financial situation at the village. Hopefully your life will return to normal with me out of the picture.

Good bye, Roberta

5 June, (Thursday)

Hi Martin

I've removed my half of the funds in our joint Commonwealth account and $576.48 from your portion to pay for the repair of my car bumper (see enclosure). This leaves $492.11 in the account. I suggest you move it to another account which will then close the account.

Roberta

6 June, (Friday)

There's some good news for a change. I got a second quote for the bumper - this time the fellow will repair it rather than replace it. His cost is $275 which is much closer to what I thought it is worth. I see that you closed out the joint account, so I will send you a cheque for the difference. R.

6 June, (Friday)

Thanks Roberta,

I have to say that I presumed the repair had been carried out and did not check that it was a quotation. When you have paid for the repair, you may find it easier to transfer the difference back into the account rather than pay for a cheque and I will then transfer it into mine to close the account.

Re the letter from Meridien I sent to you yesterday, I spoke to the only new resident that could fit the complaint and she denied everything ... even crossed her heart ... so at last I have something positive to expose their lies. I will send you a copy of my reply after next week's committee meeting. You would not believe the support I received at tonight's happy hour.

I have to say that after a full hour's conversation with Les Armstrong at 10.00 pm last night (his call) I was left with a feeling of utter confusion and lack of any constructive advice.

Cheers, M

8 June, (Sunday)

Several articles in the Sunday Mail: One entitled 'Buyback is unfair, says son' By Ryan Herrernan. [Sub-title: 'Woman 98 offered half price for retirement unit.'] It also discussed 'Inside the Grey Tsunami' and 'Retirees warned of resort pitfalls'

Another article was entitled: 'Aged care needs dose of empathy – Workout is flight of fancy.' by Terry Sweetman. An every-growing army of retirees is marching towards an uncertain twilight. 'Residents are accusing companies of profiteering, putting shareholders before the elderly'

There was also an article about Les Armstrong stating that he regrets buying his retirement village unit.

After May 28th, not one person from the village contacted me. I spent some of the time visiting my family and friends in Canada (from June 28th until July 20th) but most of the time until I moved back to the Gold Coast on August 25th was spent in isolation.

There were only two additional correspondences between Martin and I:

10 January, 2009, (Saturday) 8:17 am

Hi Martin,

I felt you might want to know that Doug is not well. As you know, ten years ago he fought and won a battle with pancreatic cancer. He has been sick most of last year and they diagnosed it as being parasites. On Christmas Eve he was hospitalised and had emergency surgery to replace a bile duct from his liver to his colon. Beside the duct they found a tumour that is malignant. He will start chemo soon. He looks like a walking skeleton, so doubt if he will survive long.

You can contact them at (gave him the information).

Roberta

29 June, 2009, (Monday) 3:41 pm

Hello Martin,

I thought you should know that Doug passed away at 6:00 pm last night. His funeral will be held at Summerville Funerals in Nerang at 3:00 pm on Friday.

It has been a long hard struggle for both of them.

Roberta

29 June, 2009 (Monday) 2:03 pm

Thanks for letting me know Roberta,

What a long painful fight he had only to lose it in the end.

I have sent my condolences to Babette.

Martin

This was the last contact I had with Martin Williams.

CONCLUSION

The Queensland Retirement Village Act, 1999 is heavily slanted in favour of the Operators rather than concentrating on the rights of the residents of retirement villages. There have been many tribunals caused by this inequity which has caused considerable grief to residents – and cost them far too much time and money to solve the disputes.

One thing that's not clearly pointed out in the Act is what happens if one of the couple die and the remaining person wants a new partner to move in with him/her. They can run into all kinds of problems. I did a word search of the Queensland Retirement Village Act, 1999 and could find no reference to a Long Term Guest Licence, so this was something that Meridien had developed and used.

I highly recommend the following:

1. That the Queensland Retirement Village Act be entirely rewritten so that the rights of the Residents are equally represented with those given to Operators. The Act does not <u>fairly</u> cover incidences where:

   a) A resident dies and the remaining spouse decides to remarry or live with a partner in their unit.

   b) A partner wants to move in without putting his/her name on the PID of the unit (without paying exit fees etc.)

   c) That 'Long Term Guest Licences' remove the clauses that absolve the Owner/Operator from being responsible for the safety of the guest while s/he is on common property in a retirement village. Therefore they would remove the following clauses from the agreement:

      3. (i) acknowledges that it occupies the Unit and resides within the Village entirely at its own risk

         (ii) releases the Operator from all liability (whether in contract, tort, by statute or otherwise however) in respect of all claims whatever relating to the use and occupation of the Unit by the Guest and the residing within the Village by the Guest

      5. Guest to Indemnify Operator

> The Guest releases and indemnifies the Operator and agrees to keep the Operator and its employees, agents and contractors released and at all times indemnified to the fullest extent permitted by law from and against all claims of every description whatever incurred by the Operator or for which the Operator may be or become liable whether in contract, tort, by statute or otherwise however and whether during or after the residing in the Village by the Guest.
>
> [The Operators have a duty of care for the safety of **anyone** that comes on their property.]

2. That potential residents proposing to move into a Retirement Village property are completely aware of how much money the Operators are really taking from them if they die or decide to sell their units.

3. That owners do not have to sell their units and buy them back if they wish to take a partner to live in their home.

4. That Queensland residents ensure that a Human Rights Act or Bill of Rights (similar to that in the ACT and other states) is ratified, so that Queensland residents can fight situations such as mine relating to defamation of character/slander.

I'm now 74 years of age and still furious at the events identified in this day-by-day account of the atrocities we faced against a huge conglomerate that was so tied up with their need to make more and more money that they forgot about the residents they should have been serving and protecting. I believe their actions were a serious form of elder abuse.

Martin Williams is the kindest, most thoughtful and considerate man I've ever met. I thought I could spend the rest of my life with him, but Michelle Smith of Meridien made it impossible for us to spend our twilight years together. It's hard to believe that I have only met this woman once, but look at the damage she has done! Shame on her and Meridien and the Queensland Retirement Village Act for allowing them to accomplish this!

NOTES *

1. Page 44: 17-12-07 – Letter from Michelle Smith, General Manager Queensland AMP Capital Meridien Lifestyle.
2. Page 44-48: 17-12-07 – Long Term Guest Licence.
3. Page 54: 20-12-07 – email from Michelle Smith.
4. Page 67-71: 10-01-08 – Our amended Long Term Guest Licence.
5. Page 71-72: 10-01-08 – Letter from Michelle Smith.
6. Page 72: 10-01-08 – Email from Michelle Smith.
7. Page 76: 11-01-08 – Email from Michelle Smith.
8. Page 77-79: 14-01-08 – Email from Michelle Smith.
9. Page 85-86: 22-01-08 – Letter from Michelle Smith.
10. Page 89-90: 05-01-08: Email from Michelle Smith.
11. Page 93-96: 10-02-08 – Letter sent to Glen Brown, CEO AMP Capital Meridien Lifestyle.
12. Page 111: 07-03-08 – Letter to Craig Dunn, CEO of AMP.
13. Page 116-117: Quotes from Human Rights Act 2004.
14. Page 117-121: Quotes from the Anti-Discrimination Act 1991.
15. Page 121-122: 19-03-08 – Letter from Glen Brown, CEO AMP Capital Meridien Lifestyle.
16. Page 122-124: Quotes from Wellington Manor PID.
17. Page 131-132: 28-07-06 – Letter to the Directors of Wellington Manor from Phil Phillips.
18. Page 132-133: 18-07-06 – Letter to Phil Phillips from Bill Manning of McCullough Robertson.
19. Page 134-137: 28-02-06 – Weekly Hansard re: Retirement Villages Amendment Bill by Jann Stuckey – Currumbin.
20. Page 144-145: 28-02-06 – Hansard Report by Mr Rogers – Redcliffe about the Retirement Villages Act.

21. Page 145-146: 10-04-08 – Letter from Glen Brown, CEO AMP Capital Meridien Lifestyle.

22. Page 146-148: 04-08 – Article in the Australian Financial News about AMP Meridien.

23. Page 151-152: 28-04-08 – Letter to Craig Dun, CEO of AMP.

24. Page 155-164: 29-04-08 – Information sent to Today Tonite Channel 7 TV.

25. Page 175-176: Quotes from the Retirement Villages Act 1999.

26. Age 177-180: 12-05-08 – Letter from Michelle Smith to the residents of Wellington Manor.

www.ingramcontent.com/pod-product-compliance
Lightning Source LLC
LaVergne TN
LVHW051519070426
835507LV00023B/3194